Unlocking
the Puzzle Box

Also by Harold Klemp

The Book of ECK Parables, Volume 1
The Book of ECK Parables, Volume 2
The Book of ECK Parables, Volume 3
Child in the Wilderness
The Living Word
Soul Travelers of the Far Country
The Temple of ECK
The Wind of Change

The Mahanta Transcripts Series

Journey of Soul, Book 1
How to Find God, Book 2
The Secret Teachings, Book 3
The Golden Heart, Book 4
Cloak of Consciousness, Book 5

This book has been authored by and published under the supervision of the Living ECK Master, Sri Harold Klemp. It is the Word of ECK.

Unlocking the Puzzle Box

Harold Klemp

Mahanta Transcripts
Book 6

ECKANKAR
Minneapolis, MN

Unlocking the Puzzle Box
Mahanta Transcripts, Book 6

Printed in U.S.A.
Library of Congress Catalog Card Number: 92-70375

Compiled by Joan Klemp and Anne Pezdirc
Edited by Anthony Moore and Mary Carroll Moore
Cover design by Lois Stanfield
Cover illustration by Diane Shelton
Text illustrations by Gary Cooper
Text photo (page x) by Bree Renz
Back cover photo by John Jenkins

Contents

vii

Foreword

The Way of the Eternal, *The Shariyat-Ki-Sugmad, Book One,* states: "The knowledge that the true, living Master gives is direct and immediate, coming from actual Soul experiences apart from the physical senses and human consciousness. His words are charged with the ECK currents surging within him. They sink into the inner self of the listener, leaving little doubt about the existence of Soul experiences."

Sri Harold Klemp, the Mahanta, the Living ECK Master travels throughout the world to give out the sacred teachings of ECK. Many of his public talks have been released on audiocassette, but others have never before been available beyond the particular seminar at which he spoke.

As a special service to the students of ECK and truth seekers everywhere, all of Sri Harold's public talks are being transcribed and edited under his direction. Now these transcripts can be study aids for one's greater spiritual understanding.

Unlocking the Puzzle Box, Mahanta Transcripts, Book 6, contains his talks from 1986–87. May they serve to uplift Soul to greater areas of consciousness.

The Living ECK Master, Sri Harold Klemp, at the ECKANKAR Creative Arts Festival in Chicago, Illinois, June 1987. In his talks worldwide, he helps unlock our closed minds so the Light and Sound of God can come in to cleanse and uplift our consciousness.

1

Unlocking the Puzzle Box

O ften our lives are like puzzle boxes, locked up so tightly that the Light and Sound of God can't come in to clean out the imperfections which have accumulated over our many years here on earth. After so long a winter with the windows shut, a spring cleaning is needed.

A Chinese Puzzle Box

I noticed a little box sitting on a lampstand in the corner of one of the meeting rooms. The box was Chinese in design, a deep maroon color, highly lacquered, and with a lock on the front. I wondered what was in it, but there were other things to do at the time so I didn't get to find out.

When I returned to the room later, the box was still there. I went over and picked it up. "I wonder what's in it?" I asked.

"Two minutes until the next meeting in the adjoining room," someone answered. But by now I was really curious. I wondered if I could get the puzzle box open in two minutes.

The Ticking Clock

Like a good story needs conflict, in spiritual matters too we find that conflict makes for an interesting life. Racing against time always makes life challenging. College students working toward a degree go through this right up until graduation, wondering along the way whether they're going to win the race or not.

With about a minute and fifty seconds to go and the clock steadily ticking, I studied the box. How could I get it open?

Quickly examining the lock, I could tell it was pretty simple—as all puzzles are, really.

I took out my felt-tip pen and tried to work it into a little hole located inconspicuously at the bottom of the lock. But the pen was too thick.

"The meeting starts in one minute and thirty seconds," said my self-appointed timekeeper.

Then I saw a ballpoint pen lying next to the box. I took it apart, removed the thin ink cartridge, and used the tip to push on the inside of the lock. It started to budge just a little bit. "What could be in this box?" I wondered out loud.

"Just over a minute left," announced the timekeeper.

The lock was stuck. I jiggled it some more, but it wouldn't open. I pulled on it and tried to pry it with the other end of the ballpoint-pen ink cartridge. It didn't work. I fiddled with it a few seconds more, and finally the lock snapped open.

I flipped open the lid, half-expecting to find a Pandora's box filled with anger, lust, greed, attachment, and vanity. This is how it feels sometimes when I open letters from people who are experiencing hard times spiritually. But sending the letter is a way for whatever is bothering them to be passed off into the ECK, the Audible Life Stream.

After all that work, the box was empty. The inside was pretty, though. It was lined with very decorative paper.

"Thirty seconds!"

I slammed down the lid, worked the lock shut, slipped the spring over the ink cartridge, put it into the pen, screwed it together, set it down on the lampstand, threw my hands up in the air, and yelled, "Done!"

"One minute and fifty seconds total time," shouted the timekeeper.

We trooped next door to the meeting with the Youth Council, where I happily told them how I'd worked out the puzzle of the locked box. I compared it to playing a video game. Each game has some kind of a limit to it—you just have so many tries before the game is over.

Degrees of Motivation

Actually, everything you do is set against a time limit. Time pressure provides a certain degree of motivation, among other things. If you don't come up with the money for your car payment by the end of the month, the loan company will repossess your car. This kind of pressure can enrich your vocabulary, change your blood pressure, and increase your waking hours each day because you can't sleep for worrying.

Time pressures can occur in any environment, even in your own home. When the wife says, "Dinner's ready," she expects the husband to come to the table. After all, she's been slaving away at the stove for quite a while.

A time problem comes up when the wife wants the husband to eat the dinner she has prepared, but he's busy in the living room watching the last inning of the World Series. He's on edge, rooting for the pitcher to strike out the batter before the end of the game. Naturally he's not real interested in food at the moment.

"Why don't you come in here before everything gets cold?" she urges, miffed that he doesn't appreciate her efforts.

"Because it's the bottom of the ninth!" he snaps, wondering about her misguided values.

So the pressures of time are always with us. The anxieties that pull at us from all sides, all the time, create spiritual ill health, which then shows up as problems in our physical health.

Tracing Symptoms to Their Causes

While driving on the freeway earlier today, I suddenly started coughing. At first I thought it might be a cold coming on. Then I did a quick mental review of the foods I'd eaten in the last day or two, wondering if that might be the cause. Before seminars I'm very careful to keep away from bread and butter and all the good things that make meals worth eating. Certain foods make it hard to speak without having to clear my throat every few minutes. But this time I couldn't think of anything that would have caused the congestion.

Then I noticed that the freeway itself lay in a basin. The way it was constructed formed a sort of crater in which the pollution settled, especially on a windless day. I realized my cough was caused by the exhaust fumes from all the rush-hour traffic.

Symptoms that seem like the onset of a cold are often caused by the pollution in the air, and at certain times we are more sensitive to these outside forces.

How the HU Song Heals

This is the Year of Spiritual Healing, and in the lives of the ECK initiates, many of the symptoms of deep spiritual illnesses are coming to the surface and passing off into the Audible Life Stream.

The Year of Spiritual Healing includes aspects other than physical health. One of the greatest overall healers is the word *HU*. The HU Chant, or HU Song, is very healing to the Soul body.

A college student from Cotonou, Benin, West Africa, and his roommate decided to hold a HU Chant once a week. Every Wednesday night, the two initiates would lock the door to their room and quietly sing HU. At first they thought it was coincidence, but they noticed that after a few minutes the other students would turn off their radios and tape players, and the dormitory would grow very quiet.

Their group of two soon increased to twelve.

One Wednesday night the dozen students gathered in the room to sing HU. The two roommates each assumed the other had locked the door, as was their habit, to discourage interruptions. The HU Chant began on time.

A few minutes later there was a knock on the door. Everyone ignored it and continued to sing HU. The visitor knocked more persistently, knowing there were people in the room. When he got no response, he turned the doorknob, trying to get in. With no success, he finally gave up and went away.

When the HU Chant was over, someone else knocked on the door and turned the knob. This time the door opened. That's when the two roommates realized that they had forgotten to lock it.

They just looked at each other and said, "Baraka

Bashad." They knew it was the Mahanta who had locked the door for the HU Chant. To them it was proof of the presence of the Master during this sacred time of healing.

The ECK uses millions of ways to show the individual that the presence of the Master is always at hand. The Mahanta is the inner force of the ECK, and this force is always present.

The outer form, known as the Living ECK Master, is a matrix. It gives an individual in the physical body something to focus his attention on. The image of the Outer Master can then be carried back home and taken into contemplation when the person does his private HU Chant or sings his secret word.

In the individual contemplation sessions, one tries to come in contact with the Light and Sound, the Holy Spirit, which we call the ECK. The Light and Sound of God is the healer. This is the doctrine of ECK.

We have our holy bible, *The Shariyat-Ki-Sugmad,* as part of the outer teachings. But nothing in the lower worlds is perfect, not even the ECK writings. No bible is without error. In these lower worlds of duality, where the good cannot exist without the bad, there is no perfection. Through the spiritual exercises, we are endeavoring to go into the worlds of perfection, to the Soul Plane and above.

A Spiritual Springboard

A woman who had been a member of ECKANKAR for only ten months went to a Regional Seminar in another state, accompanied by her eighteen-year-old son who was not an ECKist. The night before the seminar was to begin, the new ECKist went downstairs to the hotel lobby for awhile. When she went back upstairs, her son was watching television. "I'm going out to get a Coke," he said and left the room. The woman lay down on the bed and closed her eyes.

Suddenly she heard a loud ripping sound. Opening her eyes, she saw a man come hurtling into the room through a slit in the window screen and scoop up her purse. "I knew this wasn't an ECK Master," she said later.

She jumped off the bed, flung open the door, and ran out to the hallway screaming. Another ECK initiate quickly led the woman to a phone. They called the manager, who immediately sent for the police.

The son returned to the room a few minutes later to find his mother being questioned by the police. "I can't believe this," he said, shaking his head. "I leave the room for five minutes, and look what happens!"

His mother knew there had to be a deep spiritual meaning in this incident. But I've been in ECK only ten months, she thought. I'm too new to figure it out.

"Can you describe the man who came through the window?" one of the police officers asked, interrupting her reverie. She answered their questions as briefly as possible, anxious to get rid of them. She wanted to go into contemplation to ask the Inner Master what the experience meant. She just knew the break-in had an important spiritual meaning.

The next day one of the speakers at the seminar told a story about a rock that had come through her car window. At first, the speaker said, she couldn't figure out why this incident had happened, but later she realized it signified a breakthrough in her spiritual life. As the weeks passed, she found answers to her questions and insights from the ECK begin to come into her life.

The woman who experienced the break-in the night before was thrilled with the talk. "It helped explain what had happened to me," she told the speaker later.

The following day she and her son accepted a ride back home with some other ECKists. During the drive, the others began to talk about the different elements and factors of life in ECK. The new ECKist suddenly felt more and more understanding coming to her about things she had questioned in the past. She also realized that the ECK had used an incident like the break-in to announce that the Holy Spirit was coming into her life to begin giving her greater breakthroughs in spiritual unfoldment and understanding.

Rare is the individual who has the spiritual viewpoint to see a seemingly negative experience as a springboard to a higher level of understanding.

Last October 22 I announced that we were entering the Year of Spiritual Healing. Many of the ECKists took it casually—Oh, next year has a theme; isn't that nice? But it was more than a theme.

To those without the spiritual sight and hearing to know the ways of ECK, life went on as usual during the Year of Spiritual Healing. Everything seemed pretty much the way it was before. But those of you in ECK who opened in consciousness were able to see that something was beginning to change in your lives. You didn't always know exactly what those changes were, but you knew something was happening.

Seeing into the Other Worlds

An initiate wrote to me about her eighty-five-year-old mother who kept berating her about ECKANKAR. "Why are you on this path?" she'd say. "I don't understand it. What do you mean, 'a path to God'? Isn't the old way good enough for you?" The mother was obviously concerned about the spiritual welfare of her daughter.

8

It's not uncommon for those of a different religious background to feel that if they don't save you in time, you will go to hell. In the past, changing other people's beliefs was done through persecution, such as in the witch trials of Salem. If such people fail in their duty to convert you before the clock runs out, they think the Lord or some angel will say, "Because you have failed, you cannot sit at the right hand of the Lord; you will have to sit at the back of the room for all eternity." This fear drives them to try very hard to change another's belief in God to fit their own.

So, not understanding the way of ECK, this elderly woman badgered her daughter about going back to the "true" way of God.

One day the mother fell and cracked a vertebra and was no longer able to walk. The daughter took her mother into her home to care for her.

Over the following six months, the older woman began to have spiritual experiences. ECK Masters and other people came into her room at night and talked to her. Finally she told her daughter and the nurse who took care of her about these visitations.

"What do these people say?" the daughter asked, humoring her.

"They told me not to tell," the woman answered.

One morning she said to her daughter, "I saw a man last night, but I don't know who it was."

Her daughter had an idea. She got some ECK materials that had pictures of the ECK Masters and brought them to her mother. Together they studied each one.

"Did he look like this?" she asked, pointing to a picture of Gopal Das.

"No," her mother said.

"How about Fubbi Quantz?" The mother shook her head.

"Yaubl Sacabi? Rami Nuri?" It wasn't any of these.

The daughter then remembered that a recent issue of the *Mystic World* had pictures of both Paul Twitchell and the present Living ECK Master. She showed them to her mother. "Was it one of these two?"

"It was that guy there," her mother said, pointing to a picture of Wah Z. This gave the daughter comfort and assurance that her mother, who was so close to going to the other side, had the protection of the Mahanta.

For the first time, the daughter began to appreciate the older woman's sense of humor. For instance, no longer able to walk, the older woman would say, "What is this? Every night I get up and wander around the room. Tie me down, would you?"

Sometimes she would say, "What's going on? If I can walk at night, why can't I walk in the morning?"

"In the dream state you are moving about in the Soul body," the daughter explained. In those final six months, the ECKist said she learned many things about her mother that she hadn't realized before.

Those of you who have been with elderly people near the time of translation realize that they begin to see into the other worlds. When the time comes, they go out in a very natural way.

Unfortunately, people who don't understand what is happening assume that Granny's losing her mind. It's not true. It's simply that her Spiritual Eye is beginning to open to the other worlds.

My own grandmother was a sweet, kind woman. In the months just before she translated, I was about eight or nine years old. She would sit by herself in her sewing room, sometimes stitching by hand, mumbling and talking as if she were carrying on conversations with very real people. Though I couldn't see anybody, I could tell she was happy. At that young age it didn't occur to me to interfere, so I was able to allow my grandmother her space. When she had completed her life cycle, she went peacefully, in a very gentle way.

Nowadays the process of death is carefully hidden from children, so that they never see this part of the natural life cycle. They see everything from newborn babies to older people, but not the rest of the cycle. Therefore, most children today are unaware of the change in consciousness that takes place as these older people get ready to leave the body. It's a very good change.

Inner Master and Outer Master

Sometimes when people come in contact with the Outer Master, a healing occurs. Thinking that the Outer Master is responsible, they'll thank him for restoring their health. But the healing actually comes from the Inner Master, the Mahanta, which is the other side of the Living ECK Master. Together they work as a unit which we call the Mahanta, the Living ECK Master.

The ECK manifests a form on each plane in the lower worlds, and on each plane this form is known as the Outer Master.

When an individual living on the Astral Plane comes in contact with the form of the Master there, that form is just as real to him as the physical body is to you here. The individual knows the outer manifestation of the ECK as the Living ECK Master, just as you do here.

If this individual goes to the next plane up, the Causal Plane, which to him is an inner plane, he then comes in contact with the Mahanta. The Mahanta works in the invisible worlds.

Even in the higher planes, there is always the Mahanta, the Living ECK Master. On the Causal Plane, too, there

is a Master who is very much like the physical Master is
to you. There the manifested form also has the inner part,
the Mahanta, who works on the next invisible plane up,
the Mental Plane.

In the past people thought the term *Living ECK Master*
applied only to the Physical Plane, the Mahanta being on
all the inner planes. But to the residents of each plane—
the Physical, Astral, Causal and Mental planes—the outer
form of the ECK that they see is known to them as the
Living ECK Master; in the invisible planes above each
respective area is the Mahanta. The two elements always
work together. This is the balance of ECK.

A Gift of Hearing

It is important for you to know, not only in your spiritual exercises but also in the spiritual healings that come
to you in your daily lives, that I can't take credit for any
healings. And I sure wouldn't want to take credit for any
illnesses.

Illness occurs because the individual has not understood one of the basic laws of Divine Spirit. When the
understanding comes, then the illness gradually goes away
or is changed. Or sometimes it is used to develop deep
spiritual character in a person.

A man came up to me at a seminar and said, very
quietly, "I came here deaf, and now I can hear. When I
first sat down, I couldn't hear you. I've never been able
to hear before. But all of a sudden, as you were speaking,
I began to hear." Perhaps he spoke so softly because he
wasn't used to the sound of his own voice. His manner was
very humble.

It would have been nice to take credit for this healing,
but I couldn't. It happened because he had touched the

Inner Master and the healing principle. It's the same principle Jesus referred to when he said, "The Father that dwelleth in me, he doeth the works." The outer form can never take credit, for the inner principle, the ECK, the Holy Spirit, is all life. The Mahanta manifests into this particular form because it is easier for you to relate to someone in the human body, someone who can answer questions through physical means.

The Farmer and the Wood Duck

There are many different ways to look at life. When a problem comes up, we can fight it or just let nature run its course. But we often feel compelled to beat the clock: We get impatient with the natural cycle of an event and want to hurry things along.

Farmers don't get much time off, especially on a dairy farm, with the morning milking, evening milking, and endless chores in between. But one Sunday afternoon, a dairy farmer decided to take a few hours off and get some rest. He stretched out on the couch and closed his eyes, planning to take a short nap. Suddenly he heard a strange noise coming from the basement. He listened intently for a moment, but it wasn't repeated. Figuring it must be his imagination, he relaxed and drifted off to sleep.

The noise sounded again and jolted him awake. This time he jumped up and ran down into the basement to investigate. There was no one there. Wondering what it could have been, he went back upstairs and lay down on the couch.

His eyes had barely shut when he heard the strange noise again, even louder than before. Once again he ran down to the basement. He looked very carefully in all the corners. If an intruder had gotten into the house, he wanted to take care of it right then and there.

The noise seemed to be coming from the furnace. Since it was summer, the old, wood-burning furnace had not been used for some time. He opened the door and looked inside.

To his amazement, gazing out at him from the dark interior of the furnace was a soot-covered wood duck.

The farmer and the wood duck stared at each other for a moment. The duck didn't make a move to come out, and the farmer certainly wasn't about to go in after it. But he had to do something.

The farmer considered the possibilities. Finally, being the kind of person who likes to let things run their natural cycles, he decided on a course of action.

Leaving the furnace door open, he swung open the two doors that led out of the basement. Why not let the duck find its own way out to the patch of blue sky showing through the cellar doors? That done, the farmer went back upstairs to the couch and finally got some rest.

A few hours later he went back down to the basement. Just as he suspected, the furnace was empty; the sooty wood duck was gone. The farmer shut all the doors, satisfied that the problem had been solved in a natural way. Even though he was not an ECKist, he was actually working with an ECK principle.

Later he figured out what had happened. The wood duck had probably been flying along when it saw the chimney of the farmhouse and decided it would be a good place to build a nest. Wood ducks like to do this in old, hollow trees and other closed-in places. Somehow it flew down the chimney, managed to make a sharp turn where the pipe turned, made its way down about ten feet of thick pipe, and ended up in the furnace. At this point it must have panicked, wondering how it was going to get out of there. That's when it started making the noise that the farmer heard.

As I listened to this story, I couldn't help wondering what I would have done if I had been asleep upstairs, heard a noise in the basement, and found a duck in the furnace. A few years ago I probably would not have let nature take its course. Instead, I would have gotten a broom handle and started poking it around in the furnace until the duck came flying out at full speed. I could imagine it reeling blindly into the washing machine and the woodpile, which would have made it angry enough to charge at the first moving thing it saw—which would have been me.

When a person pushes a natural cycle, he is asking for trouble.

First Soul Travel Experiences

In our spiritual life we, too, lie asleep, until the Master wakes us up with some noise during the dream state that will get us off the couch. When people first come into ECKANKAR, they sometimes have slightly upsetting dreams or inner experiences. They awaken in a near world of the Astral Plane, which is almost identical to the physical world. They think they are waking up right here, but Soul is moving into the other worlds. They are really coming awake in the dream state. The phenomenon we call Soul Travel is beginning.

Soul Travel simply means the movement of Soul into higher states of consciousness. It may take the form I just described. When we, as Soul, are awakened by a noise, we jump up startled. Not yet sure that Soul is eternal and lives forever, we view any noise that comes while we lie asleep and unprotected as a threat to our physical self. Then, as we look around, all of a sudden we think, Hey,

I feel different. I feel good! And slowly the realization comes that we are on a higher plane than the physical state of consciousness.

With this higher state of consciousness comes a degree of perception, happiness, and a mental clarity beyond description. It is a state in which the individual feels natural, where he says, "This is what I am: I am Soul, I am eternal, and I would like to stay here forever." But as quickly as he says, "here forever," meaning apart from the physical body asleep on the couch, Soul returns there. It happens as soon as the attention goes back to the physical body.

Now having proof that there is life beyond the physical body, the person constantly strives to return to this higher state. It's an exciting, interesting experience, and the way to bring it about is through the spiritual exercises. When he is ready for it, the ECK chela is given this experience in the other worlds of God, in the heavens which are spoken of in the many different religions. And once he has the actual experience, he comes back the knower. I would like to think of the initiates in ECK as the knowers, not the believers. There is a world of difference between knowing and believing.

Before ECK, many of our problems from the past were locked up inside of us. During this Year of Spiritual Healing, the Mahanta came and fiddled with the lock on the Chinese puzzle box, got it open, and released the five passions of the mind—anger, greed, lust, attachment, and vanity. When these five passions are let out, one is released from them, but then he still must work out the effects. This is how the healing takes place.

Assignment in Salem

My daughter started attending a new school that had an interesting program. It allowed the English teacher and the history teacher to combine classes. This helped the students improve their writing skills as they worked with the lessons of history.

My daughter's assignment was to write about the witch trials in Salem, Massachusetts, in 1692, and what her feelings would have been if she had been singled out as a witch in those days.

That evening she sat at the table staring at a blank sheet of paper. After much agonizing, she went to her mother and said, "Mom, I can't write this. Nothing will come. I just don't know what to write."

"Don't worry, it will come," her mother said. "Sit down, and relax." She sat down and tried again.

As my daughter envisioned how it must have been during those trying times, an image from the past began to emerge and take shape. She saw herself as a young woman sitting with a group of people in front of a cozy fireplace. The house was dark but clean. The adults and children listened with rapt attention as the neighborhood storyteller related a particular incident that had happened in the community.

Suddenly there was a sharp rap on the door, and the town constable barged into the room with his assistant. The two men stomped over and stood in front of the woman. "You have been accused of witchcraft!" the constable said. The woman's eyes widened in disbelief, then terror, as she realized what she was in for next.

Without even a cloak to put over her, the accused woman was taken to prison and thrown in a cold cell, where she remained for several days before being brought to trial.

Finally the dreaded morning came when the guards arrived to escort her to the courtroom. The judge and spectators turned away from her, afraid to look into the eyes of a witch. Not even her husband would look at her.

Near the front of the room stood a young girl, about twelve years of age. The girl was her accuser.

An interesting turnabout took place then. The woman who had been unjustly accused of witchcraft suddenly turned and pointed at the girl. "The child is possessed!" she said. "This child sees me as a witch because she is possessed." Because it was believed that children possessed by the devil were often guilty of accusing innocent people of witchcraft, the trial took a whole different direction, and the woman was exonerated.

An event which had been locked within my daughter from the past came forth, and now it had to be dealt with here.

The next day she turned in her completed assignment. When she went back to class the following day, the teacher announced to her in front of the class, "Your paper is being considered for a writing contest."

Telling me about it later, she said, "Dad, I was so proud I wanted to stand up and shout, 'Wow!' But I had to keep my eyes on the desk and make believe I was humble."

The experience turned out to be a good one in that it opened up the past. As she was racing against time to meet a deadline, the Inner Master was able to come through and open up the puzzle box to the past, so that something that had been trapped in there could be released and let go. The awareness of this particular past event brought changes and freedom in the form of a greater sense of responsibility and self-direction.

World Wide of ECK, St. Louis, Missouri,
Friday, October 17, 1986

The cat wanted to get away from the minister because it was being petted in a way that didn't meet its needs.

2

The Shariyat Technique

This seminar forms a bridge between the Year of Spiritual Healing and the Year of the Arahata. This talk is also a bridge and is based on a spiritual exercise I call the Shariyat technique. It's for those who are practical in nature, who are very much into what this world has to offer. Some people are so practical, in fact, that they have a hard time going into the inner worlds. I hope this exercise will help.

Developing Spiritual Exercises

As I develop different spiritual exercises and imaginative techniques that people can use to get into higher states of consciousness, sometimes it seems I've given all the variations I can come up with. Then someone will write me saying, "I've tried them all; nothing has happened. Please help me." It's nice to hear from people who say a certain spiritual exercise has worked for them. But as long as even one person says, "Please help," this cry for spiritual assistance means we'd better come up with still another technique.

People first coming on the path of ECK sometimes

21

expect to have to change themselves to fit the teachings. They are used to religions that give truth according to a certain formula that no longer fits the times. But with the constantly changing spiritual needs of people today, I am trying to keep the ECK teachings current and fresh, to give the individual realistic help for his spiritual unfoldment toward God.

The Minister's Cat

I read a story about a minister who was stroking a fidgety cat. Surely any sensible cat would enjoy the pampering, yet this one was bristling with anger and trying to get away.

The bystander observing this scene got close enough to see why the cat was so upset: The minister was stroking its fur against the grain, from the tail up to the head.

The minister tried to calm the agitated cat, talking to it in a quiet, soothing voice. As the observer moved closer, he could hear the minister saying, "Turn around, cat. Turn around."

This story is a good parable for how some religions expect people to change their thinking to fit the old dogma, even though, for many, these outdated teachings go against the grain.

The cat wanted to get away from the minister because it was being petted in a way that didn't meet its needs. And frankly, you'll seldom meet a being more sensible than a cat.

How Pets Bring Healing

Some of us are cat people and others are dog people. I think I'm more of a cat person, although I also like dogs.

In fact, we have a little dog at home. Molly is a sweet, forgiving little animal whose main reason for being on earth is to love somebody—even a cat lover. Even the neighborhood cats come running over whenever they see us out for a walk, because our dog is very much like a cat. Maybe that's why she gets along so well in our family. She's very gentle and intelligent, but without the ornery, selfish traits of a cat. Those of you who have cats probably notice that they don't really seem to miss you too much when you're gone for the day. But dogs are different. As soon as you walk in the door they go wild with joy, trying to jump up and lick your face. With cats, you're lucky if they look up to see who let the draft in when the door opened.

Cats and dogs each give love in their own way. Pets bring healing from loneliness and are companions at times when our own kind won't have us. Sometimes pets are closer to us than our family, because they don't judge us—unless, of course, dinner's late. They need a *real* reason.

Cats and dogs have their jealousies, but they don't gossip. Generally all they want is to love and be loved. People who have a difficult time accepting love from others sometimes find it easier to accept love from a pet. This companionship offers a healing which makes life bearable for them.

When Soul takes up residence in bodies other than the human form, such as that of a dog or a cat, It's just at a different level of consciousness. But Soul in any form is from God, the SUGMAD; and God is love.

Working into Better Health

The subject of healing is usually thought to apply only to humans, but many of us know it also means taking better care of the pets who give so much love and companionship.

Molly is about twelve years old. Having been treated poorly by children when she was a puppy, her vision is damaged in one eye. But she has good spirit. For some reason buried in her past, she doesn't like bicycles. She used to chase them the way other dogs chase cars, but now that she's getting on in years she's content to let most bicycle riders go by in peace.

Several months ago Molly developed a dry cough that grew steadily worse. We found that she had the same problems with food as the two adults in our family. For me, anything made with flour causes congestion. It occurred to me that in the years I lived on the farm, I got too much of it. At some point the body developed an allergy and began to put up a resistance. So every time this particular food is taken into the body, it forms congestion to protect itself against this foreign substance which has become a poison to it.

As a person gets older the body's resistance and tolerance diminishes, and it begins to reject certain foods which it was able to handle before. But the initiate in ECK has the consciousness to change his diet as his body becomes unable to handle the foods he enjoyed in the past. Therefore, he is able to work in a better state of health than those who continue with the same diet. The people who won't make changes start to develop a number of ailments, until eventually they can't carry on anymore.

Even animals felt the impact of the Year of Spiritual Healing. And if someone in the household is going through a healing, the rest of the family get to go along for the ride, which means nobody gets any sleep. Our little dog, Molly, coughed and coughed, night after night. This went on for months. We changed her diet several times, experimenting

24

with different foods. Each new food brought a temporary improvement, but after a few days another allergy which had been lying in the background came forth.

We found a very good veterinarian who works with a natural means of healing and uses medicine only in critical situations. He said Molly's condition had reached a crisis and that it would take an antibiotic to get her past this stage. But since antibiotics are not good for the animal, he said we would soon have to try to wean her away from it, at the same time changing her diet to make her stronger. Even though we had always given her the best available diet based on the standard school of veterinary medicine, this doctor recommended a whole new dietary program. Since then, Molly has seldom had a cough.

We also worried about how this twelve-year-old dog with congestion problems, coming from the warm state of California, would take to the cold of Minnesota. We figured she'd never want to go out in the freezing weather. But as it turns out, she loves it. She goes outside and hops around like a puppy.

People who watch their pets closely can learn something about healing themselves. We found that there was a parallel between the foods that Molly was sensitive to and the foods that caused us problems. By watching her carefully we learned about ourselves. She's better now, and so are we.

The Need for a Miracle

In the Year of Spiritual Healing, there have been occasional reports of healings that would be considered miraculous. These healings happen to people who have earned them.

An ECK initiate had suffered four broken ribs while

stationed at a military base this past April. Although the breaks showed up on the X rays, there wasn't much the doctors could do. They wrapped her chest with bandages to restrict her movement while the ribs healed and released her from the hospital.

As soon as the injury was almost healed, the ECKist had another accident. A bone scan was done. The fluorescent dye injected into her body clearly showed that the same four ribs were broken again. The doctors ordered additional X rays.

It took two hours before the technicians were ready to take the X rays. The ECKist was in a lot of pain as she sat in the waiting room.

All of a sudden she felt an incredible surge of warmth surround her body. Something is going on, she thought. She went over to look out the window. Even the sun appeared brighter than usual. Something was happening, but she didn't know what.

Finally she was called in to have the X rays taken. The results were puzzling: None of the X rays showed any broken ribs. The doctors couldn't understand it; they had no choice but to send her home.

They didn't even schedule her to come back for a follow-up examination. They probably figured it would be best to just say, "Don't call us; we'll call you." For doctors on a military base who are in line for a promotion, misinterpreting tests and X rays does not look good on the record. They didn't realize that the woman had received a spiritual healing.

People would like me to give a certain formula for healing—to do a little dance, mumble the sacred words, go into deep contemplation, and lo and behold, the healing is accomplished. But there is no formula. Healings of a miraculous nature always depend upon the conditions in a person's life at that particular time. What worked for one initiate may or may not work for you.

The woman who received the healing does her spiritual exercises and serves the ECK any way she can. As one of the earlier missionaries of ECK, she traveled extensively in Its cause. She has undergone hardships which are difficult to comprehend, the greatest being loneliness. But she got through it. And when she needed one, a healing was given.

Examples like this give you an idea of how Divine Spirit works in bringing healings to those on the path of ECK. I mention personal stories about doctors and chiropractors that I have gone to simply to get some people past the idea that the spiritual leader of ECKANKAR never needs medical help. Maybe they think I sneak sips of an ancient potion that gives me secret powers.

A better way is just to find good doctors. Because of their interest in healing and serving other people, they are also coming in contact with the ECK. But even when someone recommends a doctor to you, it's best to check him out for yourself.

Effects of Different Colored Lights

Even something as simple as selecting contact lenses can get very involved. There are clear contacts and colored contacts, one processing system or another, and everybody has a philosophy or a theory about them.

In a recent visit to an eye doctor, I brought up the subject of light and the effect that colored contacts might have upon vision and health. He then told me about the research conducted by John Ott of Chicago, who gave up a thirty-year career in banking to begin a series of experiments with light. Curious about the effects of different colored lights on a person's health, he came up with some interesting discoveries.

He found that the regular lighting used in homes—the white incandescent bulb, which falls within the red end of the light spectrum—had certain disadvantages unrecognized by others in the medical field. He changed the lights in his own home to the other end of the spectrum, the blue end, using blue incandescent bulbs and fluorescent lamps.

To confirm his theory that light did have an influence on people's behavior, Ott found the ideal testing ground: two restaurants in Chicago located beneath the street level where no natural sunlight filtered down.

One restaurant had very modern decor. It was illuminated with black-light ultraviolet lights, which fall within the blue end of the light spectrum, and the waiters wore coats colored with fluorescent paint that glowed in the dark. Although this type of lighting was used only as a novelty feature to attract customers, Ott discovered that almost all the employees had worked there for eighteen years and seemed very happy with their jobs. Everybody got along well.

Right next door was another restaurant that used ordinary white lights in the pink spectrum. Ott's survey of the employees revealed that they were unhappy with their jobs, either fighting among themselves or out sick with one ailment or another. None seemed to stay longer than two or three months.

Ott was so astonished with these findings that he followed up with a number of other studies. He wanted to determine the specific effects of the ordinary pink-spectrum white light bulb used in most homes and offices. Though there were some apparent health benefits, he was especially interested in the harmful effects that hardly anyone realized—the damage to health, to nerves, and to feelings of goodwill.

I'm not necessarily endorsing his theories. Anyone who has an open mind and is willing to experiment can find out for himself.

ECK Health Professionals

During this Year of Spiritual Healing, first steps were taken to draw together the medical professionals among the ECKists. Many of these people are interested in finding new spiritual insight as they bring relief to those who not only want to be healed, but to understand the causes of their sickness. If those seeking healings realized how these illnesses came about, they could take steps to help themselves.

Softening Your Attitudes

An initiate had a sudden onset of severe headaches and stomach pains. Only after the pain became almost too great to bear did the sufferer realize the tie-in with a karmic condition caused by a certain attitude she had developed years ago.

The individual called her father, a doctor who lived in another town, and described her symptoms.

"It sounds like you're suffering from migraines," he said.

The headaches had come on so quickly that she hadn't even considered that possibility.

One evening during contemplation, the reason for these severe headaches came to her. Her pain had opened up a childhood memory of her mother. Her mother had suffered with migraines. The pain was so severe that she became addicted to drugs, and for all these years the daughter had resented her mother for this weakness.

Suddenly, within a very short period of time during the Year of Spiritual Healing, the same condition that had caused her to feel such resentment toward her mother finally came to the surface.

The Spiritual Exercises of ECK gave her strength as Soul to understand and, more importantly, to accept the reason for her pain. She could now look at herself honestly and admit that she had formed a negative attitude simply because she didn't understand the severity of her mother's pain; she had lacked the experience by which to gauge it.

From that point on her condition began to improve, and at last report, the migraines were gone.

Dropped from the List

Another ECKist used to wake up not knowing if he was in the dream state or here; that's because the near worlds of the Astral Plane appear very similar to the Physical Plane. The only way he could prove to himself that he was in a higher state of consciousness on the Astral Plane was by putting his hand through physical objects, such as a door or a table. He got quite a kick out of this.

In one of these experiences, several people came into the room to watch him, cheering and applauding each time he put his hand through a piano or table or wall. For a while he really enjoyed all the attention.

Suddenly the realization that he was merely performing silly tricks made him sick. Why am I doing this? he wondered. What am I doing here?

"Go away!" he yelled to the group of observers.

To his surprise, everyone seemed very pleased that he had stopped playing games. As soon as he realized this, he began to rise upward. He passed through a number of different planes, worlds of stars and other beautiful places.

Eventually the face of a clock appeared in front of him, and he knew he was being given wisdom about the nature of time.

All of a sudden he heard a great booming voice. "I am the ruler of hell!" it said. "If you go any higher, I will drop you from my list!"

The dreamer immediately recognized the speaker as the Kal Niranjan, ruler of the lower worlds. This being, often known as Satan, serves as the educator of Souls in the lower planes.

Though the Kal's words sounded like a threat, the traveler had to laugh out loud at the irony of the situation. For if Soul continued to move into the higher worlds, then indeed It would be dropped from the Kal's list—no longer included in the recording angel's book, no longer bound by past-life karma.

As Soul, he had gone through these lower-world life experiences so many times that there was nothing left to be frightened about. But the nature of God, the SUGMAD, was something quite different. To the dreamer, the regions above the Kal's domain were still the great unknown. It came to him that the Kal was trying to frighten him into staying in the lower worlds, to protect him from this great unknown.

Such a journey can be a little scary, but is a fitting experience for an adventurer who knows within himself that his mission and destiny are to learn what lies in these worlds beyond form.

The Shariyat Technique

I want to do everything possible to give you insight into how the process of healing occurs. If a healing is not to come directly, as in the case of the four broken ribs, it generally comes by raising your consciousness through the spiritual exercises. From the viewpoint of the higher consciousness you can recognize what is causing you to enjoy less than the quality of health you deserve at this particular time in life.

This exercise is for people who are so practical and down-to-earth that they don't have too much success with the imaginative techniques geared to finding the Light and Sound of God.

The first step is to define the problem that has been bothering you, whether it's a matter of health, finances, or love. Then put it into the form of a question: Why is this situation a problem in my life?

Next, open *The Shariyat-Ki-Sugmad,* Book One or Two, at random. Read a paragraph, then close your eyes. Chant HU eight times, which corresponds to the eight outer initiations. It doesn't matter if you're sitting up or lying down. Then, for about five minutes, go into quiet contemplation of the paragraph you just read.

Chant HU eight more times, then continue your quiet contemplation of the paragraph.

Do this a third time: Chant the HU about eight times, then contemplate for about five more minutes.

The entire contemplation will take from fifteen to twenty minutes.

Open *The Shariyat* at random again, and read another paragraph. See how this paragraph relates to the first paragraph; how both offer a new insight and approach to your problem. It may tell you the next step to take.

Usually a problem lingers because we are afraid to take the first step toward resolving it. Four or five different possibilities may come to mind, but because we don't know which one is best and we're afraid of failure, we put off doing anything.

Once the Shariyat technique helps you determine your next step, if necessary you can repeat it again the second night to carry the solution a step further. Or you can use it on another problem that may be bothering you. See if you get some new direction or new perspective on the situation.

There will be other side benefits to this exercise, which you can find out for yourself.

May the blessings be.

World Wide of ECK, St. Louis, Missouri,
Saturday, October 18, 1986

In ECK we are eagles, and we recognize that it is our own kind who walk the heavens. Once we accept responsibility for ourselves, we no longer unconsciously react to the emotions and will of others.

3

Eagles in ECK

There is a story among the Blackfoot Indians about an Indian brave who came across an untended eagle's nest while climbing a steep cliff. He managed to remove one of the eggs and carry it back to his village. He placed the egg in a hen's nest until it hatched. Thus was born into the world the little eaglet who thought it was a chicken.

An Eagle's Story

Following the example of the mother hen, the young eagle learned to walk with its head lowered to the ground, scratching in the dirt, pecking at worms and seeds.

One day when the eagle was fully grown, he looked up and saw a magnificent bird soaring across the heavens.

"What is that?" he asked his family.

"That's an eagle," answered the old grandma hen, who knew many things about the world.

"How wonderful it must be to fly so high," he said.

"Yes, it must be," she agreed. "But forget it. You're a chicken."

So without further question, the eagle lived out the rest of his life a chicken, scratching in the dirt.

In ECK we are eagles, and we recognize that it is our own kind who walk the heavens. Once we accept responsibility for ourselves, we no longer unconsciously react to the emotions and will of others. We learn to be the active cause in life, rather than the effect of other people's limitations and efforts to control us. That is the difference between being free and being a slave.

First Day of School

The first day of school was a big day for my daughter. She was new in school, and not knowing anyone, she felt a bit uneasy, wondering what the school would be like. Were her clothes all right? Would she fit in?

When it was time for history class, she took her seat among sixty other students. Suddenly the door at the front of the classroom opened, and in walked Mr. Davis, the history teacher. He looked frantic. Right behind him came the principal, a quiet, gentle-looking woman.

"Mr. Davis, we really must talk about your class schedule," she said.

"I don't want to talk about it," Mr. Davis snapped. "I've had enough." He threw his books on the desk and went to the blackboard. Grabbing a piece of chalk, he began to scribble out the class outline for the day.

The principal was patient but persistent. "Mr. Davis, we really must talk," she said. "We can't put this off any longer."

Mr. Davis flung the chalk against the blackboard. "I can't take any more," he screamed. "I quit! I'm leaving!" With that he turned and stomped out the door.

The children watched the scene in wide-eyed shock. "Oh, wow, this is really good," they whispered among themselves, snickering nervously. My daughter opened one of her textbooks in front of her face and peeked around it, trying not to giggle out loud. The principal quickly marched the students off to study hall. From there they went to the rest of their morning classes, then to lunch.

After lunch they went to English class, and there they got quite a surprise. Seated at the front of the classroom, his feet propped up on the desk, calmly chewing an apple, was none other than Mr. Davis. The children just looked at him as they filed in the door, not knowing what to think.

Primary Source

When everyone had taken a seat, the teacher stood up and looked at the faces before him. "How many of you thought what you saw this morning in history class was real?" he asked. Almost everyone's hand went up. He went on, "Today I'm going to explain the difference between a primary source and a secondary source."

Blank looks. What on earth was this man talking about?

He asked a number of the students to describe what they had seen. Each one reported the details just a little bit differently. He then instructed the class to write a one-page report of the incident as they had seen it.

When they had finished writing their reports, he began to explain. "A primary source of information is when you yourself were there," he said.

He asked the class if they had talked with any of the other students during the lunch hour about the morning's incident. Several kids nodded yes. They said they had heard a lot of talk around the school from others who hadn't been there.

"What did the others say?" he asked.

They told him of several different versions they had

heard about the episode, none being as accurate as what they had witnessed in class firsthand.

"That's because you and your reports are the primary source of information," he said. "The reports of those who heard it secondhand are secondary sources."

With this example, he was able to get across to the children a complicated principle. The idea was to teach them that their own experience always has the most validity, even if their perceptions of an event differ from those of others. He also wanted them to learn how to become involved in what they saw. The writing assignment was an exercise in reporting from the central-character position, which was how he wanted them to do their reports for the rest of the semester.

A Principle to Live By

The difference between a primary and a secondary source is the difference between knowing and faith. In ECK we live our lives according to the principle of the primary source. To us, the way to truth is through personal experience, here on the physical plane as well as in the inner worlds. This is how we learn what life is all about and what truth means to us individually.

Those who are willing to accept the so-called truths of life from others, from secondary sources, are content to go on faith. In teachings where the emphasis is on faith, they are actually saying, "Take my word for it: This is what occurs in heaven; this is the nature of the Holy Spirit or God. You can't know for yourself until after this life is over." This is the principle of the secondary source.

Once you are aware of the difference between the primary and the secondary source, you can consciously choose the principle by which you want to live your life.

Personal Initiative

Sometimes we find ourselves thrown unwillingly into a new experience, a primary-source condition. This is the nature of life. We learn the most when put into a new situation that doesn't allow us to rely on past methods or experiences.

On a trip to Houston a few weeks ago, my schedule was so hectic that I decided to order dinner from room service rather than go out to a restaurant. This gave me a chance to get a few more things done.

The food was delivered to the room by a young man. While I was signing the bill, I asked him how things were going on his job. I'm always curious about people.

"Very well," he said.

"How long have you worked here?" I asked.

"Four days."

"Have you learned much about the job in four days?" I asked, wondering if anything worthwhile could be learned in such a short time.

He said, "The guy who's training me is out sick today, so I'm working alone and having to figure things out for myself."

"What kind of things?"

He thought for a moment before answering. Then he said, "I've learned that you have to do it yourself." This knowledge was obviously based on actual experiences.

In ECK, the process of learning to do it yourself is always tempered by learning to do it with the help of the Mahanta, the ECK, or Divine Spirit—however you think of It—even though it may appear to others you are acting by yourself. Only when we become capable of taking care of ourselves and willing to do things on our own initiative are we truly fit to become Co-workers with God.

Expanding Your Abilities

During this Year of Spiritual Healing I have gone to a number of different medical professionals. I learned from each of them, but the ones I stayed with were those who showed a true interest in healing. They earned a good living, but they didn't put moneymaking first, with healing being merely a good way to do it. Their primary concern was healing the patient.

A chiropractor was asked if he did adjustments on pets. He hadn't ever thought about it before, but he said, "A vertebra is a vertebra. Bring your pet in and let's see."

His first animal patient was a cat. "It's a show cat," its owner explained. "The only problem is that its tail has begun to droop." She placed a proud, regal-looking feline on the adjustment table. Its tail had a very unregal droop.

The woman said, "I've taken it to veterinarians. I've tried relaxants and all kinds of antibiotics, but nothing works." As a last resort, she decided to try a chiropractor. If he could make the tail go back up, she could enter the cat in shows again.

At first the chiropractor was puzzled—he hadn't ever done this before. But as he examined the cat, he noticed that the tail appeared to be an extension of the coccyx or tailbone. On that basis he began to make a few adjustments. Suddenly, just like that, the cat's tail shot straight up in the air.

"I was really surprised it worked," he said later.

Because this man was able to recognize the similarity in the structure of humans and animals, his ability didn't have to stop at a certain point. He didn't allow limitations to obstruct him in his profession. With his wide viewpoint of life he sees his role as that of a healer, rather than just as a chiropractor who can work only on human beings.

A person like this is the active, or primary, source—someone who likes to make things happen instead of being the one they happen to. Such a person likes to take charge and figure out the solution, even if it appears unorthodox. If you can find a doctor like this, you are very fortunate. If you can *be* such a person, you are even more fortunate.

Each of you has the potential and the capability to become much more than you are now. Once you open yourself to the Holy Spirit within, you can become an eagle in ECK, the experienced being, fully trained and qualified to become a Co-worker with God.

Request for a Healing

A dental hygienist had been a member of ECKANKAR for about two months when she received information in the mail about an upcoming ECK seminar. She really wanted to attend. She had only enough money to pay the preregistration fee, but she quickly made up her mind to find a way to earn enough to cover her travel expenses. "If the ECK wants me to be at the seminar," she said, "It will help me to find a way."

She previously had registered her name with a temporary agency, hoping for extra work, but they hadn't called her in seven months. The day after she decided to go to the seminar, the agency called. "If you are interested, we have work for you at a dentist's office," she was told. "It will be a short-term job, just until they can hire a permanent employee." The ECKist was delighted.

She reported for work the following morning and soon became friendly with the receptionist. As they chatted during a break, the receptionist said, "I've got a tremendous headache."

The new ECKist commented that she used to read palms and do healings.

41

"Can you heal me and give me a reading?" the receptionist asked.

But the ECKist had learned of the harm that could come to a healer, unless the healer knew how to turn the condition over to Spirit. A healer who doesn't know this unconsciously accepts the person's karma, thereby curing the illness; but later in life the healer ends up with serious health problems.

The ECKist wasn't sure how to respond to her new friend's request for a healing and a reading. She didn't want to begin on the path of ECK with the practices of the past. Having recognized their limitations, she had outgrown all that. She now wanted to follow the teachings of ECK.

The dentist came in and interrupted her thoughts. "Would you develop this X ray, please?" Grateful for the extra time to think, she immediately took the X ray into the darkroom and began the developing process. But the question kept running through her mind: What should I do? Finally she whispered, "Mahanta, please give me some sign that I am to go the ECK way."

After a while she heard someone pounding on the door. "Hey, did you go to sleep in there?" the dentist called. She hurried out with the X ray, still waiting for a sign.

"There's a streak of light across the X ray," the dentist said. "This has never happened before. There's no leak in the camera." He couldn't figure out what had caused it. But the ECKist knew it was a sign that the ECK was with her, guiding her.

From Faith to Experience

When she went back to the front office, the receptionist grabbed her arm. "Please," she said, "can you heal my headache now?" The woman was obviously in great distress.

The ECKist had actually hoped for a graceful way out of this dilemma. She still wasn't sure what to do. Finally she said, "Would you rather have a healing or a reading? You can have one or the other."

You'd think this woman with a severe headache, who had a healer standing right in front of her, would make the logical choice. But she said, "Give me a reading." People tend to lose track of their immediate concerns and ask for the wrong thing.

"OK," the ECKist said reluctantly, figuring she could always go to an ECK Spiritual Aide and repent.

Still in the consciousness of a brand-new member of ECKANKAR, she didn't yet realize that, unlike many other religions, in ECK we don't work on the principle of sin, so there is no need to repent. Instead, we work in the area of total responsibility for all of our actions. No matter what we do, we must be willing to be fully responsible for every reaction we cause. This greater sense of responsibility is the only way to become a Co-worker with God.

The ECKist gave the receptionist a very brief reading, just one or two sentences. She then surrendered the other woman's headache to the ECK, rather than taking the condition on herself. A short time later the receptionist informed her that the headache was gone.

Over the next few weeks, as the two women got to be closer friends, the receptionist wanted to know more about ECK. The dental hygienist gave her books on the teachings of ECK and showed her how to chant HU. When a permanent employee was finally hired, the ECKist left. Her final paycheck was exactly the amount she needed to go to the ECK seminar.

Later she realized that two things had occurred at the

dentist's office. First, the receptionist was ready to learn about ECK, and through this acquaintance, she did. Second, the new ECKist needed to learn to trust in the Holy Spirit, and through this experience, she had.

Sometimes you take the first tentative steps in ECK out of faith, but soon you become the knower. No longer do you merely hope or believe the ECK is working for you. You now have personal proof of Spirit, the Light and Sound, in your daily life.

"She's in God's Hands"

Some spiritual healings do occur under seemingly miraculous circumstances.

An ECKist in California was preparing to move to another state. Her son made arrangements to rent a truck to move her belongings. In his conversation with the rental agent, he mentioned that his mother was looking for a real estate agent in the area to sell her home. The rental agent just happened to know someone.

That very afternoon the ECKist went to visit the real estate agent. She liked him right away and felt comfortable listing her home with him.

A question came up later about the real estate transaction, so she called his home. His wife answered and said he wasn't in. As the two women chatted, the agent's wife began to tell the ECKist about something that had happened to her daughter. She had tried to discuss it with relatives, but they wouldn't listen, preferring to brush it off as mere coincidence.

The real estate agent's daughter had fallen into a coma and had to be rushed to the hospital by ambulance. The doctors found that her lungs were filled with fluid. They placed her in the intensive care unit with plans to drain some of the fluid from her lungs the following morning.

Throughout the night the mother sat at her daughter's bedside. Sometime during the night, a priest walked into the room. He sat down and began to talk with her. She asked him who he was and where he was from. Though a Catholic, she didn't recognize his name or that of his parish.

The priest talked with her for a long time, looking intently into her eyes. Just before he left he said, "Your daughter will be healed. She is in God's hands."

In the morning the woman asked one of the nurses, "Who was that priest who came in here last night?"

The nurse looked confused. "Nobody came in here last night," she said. Anyone who is familiar with hospitals knows that the intensive care unit is carefully monitored; visitors are only allowed in with permission. The nurse had seen no one come in.

The woman never did find out any more about the mysterious visitor.

When the doctors examined her daughter that morning, they found no trace of fluid in her lungs. All symptoms were gone.

This unexplained healing was especially meaningful to the real estate agent's wife, who herself was suffering from multiple sclerosis. Her daughter's experience gave her hope for her own recovery. Being able to talk it over with the ECKist helped her to realize that a power beyond the limited knowledge of man and science could intervene here on earth.

The ECKist had come in contact with this real estate agent's wife through a seemingly coincidental chain of events. Yet through this experience the ECKist began to see the hand of ECK working through her, reaching out to give an understanding about the ways of Spirit to someone who had never heard of ECK before.

Guidance on the Fate of a Manuscript

To work with the eagle principle is to work in states of consciousness beyond the human state. Some time ago, I was reviewing a manuscript on dreams. The author was a Christian minister who had good insight into dreams. Eighty percent of the material presented the ECK principles, but the other 20 percent was interwoven with the influences of psychic paths and traditional religious dogma.

As I read through his manuscript, I knew we couldn't publish it in its present form; there was just too much in there that was not up to the standards of the ECK teachings. I thought about approaching the author to rewrite the questionable parts so that his material would represent the ECK viewpoint more accurately.

The manuscript gave a technique for remembering dreams. I decided to try it that night to see how it compared with the ECK techniques.

It didn't work.

I went to see the author on the inner planes. "Doctor," I said, "your technique doesn't work."

"So use your own," he replied.

When I awoke the next morning, his manuscript was still on my desk where I had been reading it the day before. It was a thick one, about an inch and a half. I decided to go into contemplation to see whether or not I should ask this man to do some rewrites so that we could publish it.

My desk is located away from the windows so the papers won't get blown around by the breeze. But as I started to leave the room, a gust of wind that seemed to

46

come from nowhere began to stir the top pages of the manuscript. Then very neatly, one after another, the first seven pages peeled off the stack and landed facedown right on the seat of my chair.

By turning a representative sample facedown, the ECK was saying, "This manuscript is not for you."

I went into contemplation to verify what I had been shown outwardly. The answer was definite and clear. I returned the manuscript to the author with blessings and wished him well.

Opening the Door of Soul

Each of us is a unique individual, with our own peculiar combination of experiences accumulated over many lifetimes. The truth of ECK comes to each of us like a special key, custom-designed with millions of little notches and grooves. It is the only key that will fit the lock, turn it, and open the door of Soul.

During the ECK seminars, you can pick up the inspiration to find this key for yourself. If you can take the inspiration into contemplation, you can build the spiritual strength and understanding to accept the ECK as It speaks to you every moment of every day. The ways in which the ECK works are limitless.

A Love Stronger than Death

A European ECKist wrote me about his elderly parents. One day his father suffered a stroke and was taken to the hospital. Initially he lost the ability to speak or write, but to his doctor's surprise, within a week he had recovered both of these abilities.

Right after the man came home from the hospital, still

very weak, his wife was diagnosed as having a terminal illness. This time she was admitted to the hospital while her husband remained home. The couple, who had been married for forty years, missed each other very much.

The ECKist's mother was very comfortable with life. She accepted the fullness of love as being more important than any threat; thus, death held no fear for her. In fact, her calmness about her situation made quite an impression on the doctors. They weren't used to seeing a terminally ill patient with such serenity, the serenity of Soul. It carried her through what most people would consider a terrible tribulation.

Though not an ECKist, the elderly woman was a natural Soul traveler. On her second day in the hospital she told her son, "Last night I imagined I was home in bed with your father." By using this technique to imagine herself in familiar surroundings with someone she loved, she was actually able to be with her husband.

The ECKist thought about what his father had said to him that very morning, "It felt like your mother was beside me in bed last night." His sadness was lessened by the knowledge that the bond of love his parents had shared for so many years would continue even now.

As the days passed, the husband and wife were often together, and the man now began to have experiences with the Sound of ECK. "I can hear the sound of birds chirping," he said. "I've never heard birds with such clarity before. I can even tell the various sounds made by the different kinds of birds."

This is one of the many different ways in which the Holy Spirit announces Its presence to an individual. The music of the flute, the sound of running water, or a high-pitched whistle are some of the other indications that Soul is hearing the Holy Spirit. The Sound is perceived differently at each level of consciousness.

The ECKist's mother translated, or died, ten days after being admitted to the hospital. Just before she left the body, she visited her husband on the inner planes. She told her husband, "I'm going to be busy for the next three days, so I won't be able to come and see you. I have to register in certain areas on another plane, just the way you do when you go to a different country."

On the fourth morning following her death, the elderly man said to his son, "I saw your mother last night. She was young and beautiful and dressed in her nurse's uniform, just the way she was when we met during World War II."

The ECKist had been laid off from work since his father first became ill. His lack of employment had only added to his worry.

Shortly thereafter, the ECKist was walking past his father's room. Seeing his father's eyes open, the ECKist went into the room to sit with him. "It's all right," said the son. "It's only me." His father glanced up at him for a moment, then looked past him, as if watching someone else come into the room. Suddenly his eyes opened wide in happy amazement. A short time later he quietly left the body to go into the higher worlds of Spirit.

The ECKist was now grateful that his layoff from work had allowed him to witness a very significant spiritual moment in life. To him, this experience was proof that love transcends death.

Eagles in ECK

I would encourage you to be eagles in ECK, to recognize your heritage as a spiritual being able to rise at will into the higher planes of God. When you walk with the Mahanta by your side, you are letting the highest principle in life direct you to the experiences you need. The nights are always followed by the days; sorrow is always followed by happiness.

The ultimate happiness comes when you are able to move into the higher planes consciously, and then move back and forth between the visible and the invisible worlds as a Co-worker with God.

This is your destiny; this is your mission.

World Wide of ECK, St. Louis, Missouri,
Sunday, October 19, 1986

After you have gone through the stage of taking in as much as you can about ECK, at some point the coin turns and a transition occurs: You find that you, too, are called on by the Mahanta to begin serving your fellowman.

4

"Did We Really Let Go?"

When we first come into ECK, we read the books, study the discourses, attend classes, and just take in as much as we can. But generally after the Second Initiation, a change takes place within ourselves: Soul becomes aware that It has to begin to give.

Experiencing the Higher Worlds

As we go further along in our unfoldment through the ECK initiations, we participate more and more in the Sound and Light of ECK. Even at the Second Initiation, Soul may take a journey to the Soul Plane. It doesn't become established at that plane, but It can visit. A Third, Fourth, Fifth, or Sixth Initiate may also move beyond the level of his present initiation. Although he can journey into the higher reaches of God as a visitor, he is not yet a resident.

Periodically, in the midst of these various journeys something disquieting occurs. The individual seems to go into a void, cut off from the Light of life, Itself. There appears to be a separation from the Light and Sound of God—and it worries him. He might speculate on the reasons why this Life Force seems to be cut off from him, but usually he would be wrong. Why has the ECK stopped flowing? he wonders.

At each major step in our unfoldment, with each initiation, the coin turns. The rules that applied during the Second Initiation are suddenly changed at the Third. When you finally get comfortable with the rules for the Third level, you reach the Fourth. Once again you find that you have to learn a new way of doing things.

As you go into the higher initiations and approach the area of becoming an ECK Master, you are occasionally given a taste of what it is like to be an ECK Master. Part of this is entering the great void, the endless world. Here you may experience a great amount of Light and Sound or you may have absolutely none, leaving you with the feeling in the physical consciousness that somehow you have failed.

But this is the point where the coin is turning again: No longer should you expect to bathe in the Sound and Light, the two aspects of God, for now you are actually becoming the Light and Sound, Itself. Why? Because now you are serving the SUGMAD, or God, with love.

Why Is There Conflict?

Everything in life that has any meaning comes with conflict. A writing instructor once tried to tell me that I had to put conflict into my stories. "Until you do," he would say, "there is no story." But my understanding of the ECK teachings at that time led me to say, "No, with ECK there can be no conflict."

I had conflict all around me, but I blithely tried to ignore it. Whenever anything went wrong, I just fixed my attention on the ECK and said, "These things shall pass." And when they passed, I promptly forgot about them. My understanding was off, but that attitude did help to start tomorrow with a clean slate.

Giving service means, "What can I do for you?" Bureaucratic offices sometimes misinterpret it to mean that you, the citizen, must serve me, the government. Often in ECK we get it backward, too. But if we are patient— and even if we are not—things have a way of falling into place.

A few weeks ago I went to the post office to arrange to have my mail held for about a week while I was on a trip. "Shall I fill out any forms?" I asked the postal clerk.

"You don't have to bother," he said. He was a very pleasant young man. "We'll hold all your mail until you come in to pick it up." How nice to have everything handled so easily, I thought.

Last week, just before I left for this trip, I checked at the post office again. There was a different clerk behind the counter this time, but I figured the routine would be the same. "I'm going to be out of town for a couple of weeks," I informed the clerk. "I know I don't have to fill out any forms, but I just wanted to arrange for you to hold my mail."

"Oh, yes, you do have to fill out a form," she said, handing me one.

"But the last time I came here, one of the clerks in this very post office said I didn't have to."

"That must have been Michael," she said, shaking her head. "He's always taking shortcuts. You can't do that, but he just keeps trying." Obviously she had been on the job much longer than the obliging young man from my previous visit.

A Good Deed

I figured that was the last time I would be going to the post office for a couple of weeks, but the next morning I decided to mail some packages. Behind the counter was the nice young man who had waited on me in my first visit. I was pleased to see him. He was so easy to work with, unlike the woman who had been on duty the previous day. I suspected that her hand was never far from the postal-regulations book, seeking out reasons to wag her finger at those young clerks who had funny notions about serving the customer.

"I'd like to mail these packages," I said. "Two of them have books, and the other two have books and magazines."

"The books can be sent with the cheaper special-fourth-class rate," he said, "but the others will have to go third class, which costs more. That's because magazines have advertising in them."

"These are nonprofit magazines," I quickly said. "There are no ads in them."

"Well, there are other regulations, too," he said, and proceeded to cite things like twenty-five pages or more and other requirements that precluded the cheaper rate.

"I understand," I said.

He used the special-fourth-class stamp on the first two packages and set them aside. Then he reached for the other two. Hesitating for a moment, he looked up at me and said, "Nonprofit, huh?"

"Yes," I said.

"This could be the time to do my good deed for the day," he said.

It could be, I thought.

"Oh, what the heck," he finally said, and stamped them with special-fourth-class postage.

My conflict was this: Though I don't mind paying the right price, I didn't want to interfere with his experience. This *is* work for the ECK, I figured, so why not let him charge the special-fourth-class rate? The clerk had his conflict in trying to work with the strict rules of his employer. At first, all he could do was give me two rates. But without knowing it, he found himself responding to the ECK love: He just felt there was a good reason to make this the time to do his good deed for the day. The resolution made him feel good, and it definitely made me feel good: an example of conflict, and conflict resolved.

Asking about ECK

Three ECKists were driving home from the World Wide of ECK in St. Louis. Spotting a little restaurant and store, they decided to make a rest stop. Inside the store, the friendly proprietor struck up a conversation.

"Where are you from?" he asked them. They told him they were from Wisconsin. "Are you on vacation?" he asked.

"We went to an ECKANKAR seminar," one of them answered.

"What's an ECKANKAR seminar?"

They explained a little bit about ECKANKAR and offered to give him a book.

"No, thank you," he said and quickly changed the subject.

So now the three ECKists had a conflict of sorts. A Soul had asked for more information about this path to God, but the conversation had reached a dead end. What should they do next? For lack of a better idea, they decided to get in the car and continue on home.

Just then the door burst open, and a man came hurrying into the store. Seeing the three ECKists standing by the checkout counter, he went right over to them. "I just noticed a sign in the window of a car outside. It says 'Baraka Bashad.' The license plate says HU-EVER," he said. "Are you three in that car?"

They said they were.

"Are you ECKists?" he asked.

"Yes, we are," they answered.

"I've read a little bit about ECKANKAR, and I want to know more," he said.

The proprietor just stood there listening while the three ECKists explained more about ECKANKAR to the young man who had just come in.

"Do you have any brochures?" the young man asked. "Where can I get a book?"

"Here you go," one of the ECKists said, taking a book from her purse and handing it to him.

Suddenly the proprietor had a change of heart. "I want a book, too!" he chimed in.

Resolving Conflict

In this case, Soul wanted to know about ECK, but when the information was offered too quickly, there was a conflict: ECKANKAR wasn't an orthodox teaching, so why put his own religious beliefs at jeopardy? The ECKists had their own conflict: The proprietor had given them an opportunity to be vehicles for ECK, but he was afraid to pursue the matter. Seemingly by coincidence, the ECK then arranged for another person to come into the store at just the right time and bring up the subject in a way that caught the proprietor's interest. So once again, we have conflict and conflict resolved.

If you hope to be a writer or give ECK talks, keep in mind that conflict and the way it is finally worked out through the means of Spirit is what puts meaning into a story.

Touching Another Soul

An ECKist in her mid-forties went back to college to get a degree in music. Finding herself in classes with students from eighteen to twenty-one, she naturally felt a bit out of place.

One day the students were given the assignment to choose a song and perform it for the rest of the class. Initially she selected a song from a Broadway musical, but the night before her presentation to the class, she decided to change it to one she had sung at an ECK seminar.

When she got to class, she prefaced her song by first explaining to the other students some of the ideas behind the words. She talked about out-of-body travel; Soul Travel; the Mahanta, the Living ECK Master; and the other ECK Masters. She couldn't help noticing a lack of interest in the faces of the students as she discussed these different terms; yet the Inner Master had prompted her to sing this song about ECK.

Most of her classmates wouldn't even look at her as she sang. When the song was over, no one said a word; they just quietly got up and left. The ECKist walked out of the room by herself.

The next day, as she was leaving the class, a young woman came up to her. "I liked that song you sang yesterday," she said.

The ECKist looked at her in surprise. "As I began to sing it," she said, "I could see that the class was disappointed. They would have preferred something livelier."

"Why did you choose that song?" her classmate asked.

"Because I felt I had to sing the song that told of my

experience of coming in contact with the Light and Sound of God," the ECKist said. "If anyone else in the class ever had an out-of-body experience and came in contact with these two aspects of the Holy Spirit, they might not have known what was going on. I figured this song would be a shortcut for someone, sometime."

The young woman said, "Then the person you sang it for was me." For some time now, she explained, she had been having out-of-body experiences, with absolutely no knowledge of what they meant. As she fell asleep the night before the class in which the song was sung, she had asked for an understanding of these strange experiences. The next day in class, she got her answer.

The ECKist, who had felt like an alien among the younger people, now realized how important it was to follow the nudges of the Inner Master, no matter what. It was always for a constructive purpose.

Called On by the Mahanta

After you have gone through the stage of taking in as much as you can about ECK, at some point the coin turns and a transition occurs: You find that you, too, are called on by the Mahanta to begin serving your fellowman.

The farther you go in your ECK initiations, the more you will find yourself serving, helping, and being among people. You'll carry the message of the Light and Sound of God in whatever way is needed at a particular time. Sometimes you'll do this without even talking about ECK. The ways of ECK are often quiet. When you are being used as a channel, you may never know exactly what was accomplished through you.

Listen to the Mahanta whenever the instruction comes. You will be given only uplifting and constructive projects to do, never anything destructive. If destructive ideas come through, then disregard them, because they are wrong; they are not coming through your clear inner channels. ECK is an uplifting and a building force, and there is no greater joy than working as a Co-worker with God.

A Jolt in the Marketplace

During an ECKANKAR seminar in New Orleans, an ECKist and two companions went out for a walk in the old section of the city. She was looking up, admiring the wrought-iron railings on the balconies, when another woman came hurrying along the sidewalk. The ECKist and the other woman ran right into each other. Reeling from the collision, they both reached out to steady one another.

Something unexpected happened then. The stranger grasped the initiate's hand tightly and clung to it for a long moment, which seemed to last forever.

After the two women parted, the ECKist went back to her hotel room and went into contemplation. She suddenly sensed that a great load of karma had been lifted from her. She realized it had happened when the woman bumped into her on the sidewalk. The jolt had jarred loose the karma. The initiate felt very lighthearted. She didn't realize that when karma is taken away, it leaves a vacuum within. That vacuum must be filled with something else. Not other karma, because as we go further along on the path, we realize that good and bad karma are replaced by ECK love. This is what was going to take place.

Later that day she went to an ECK workshop on spiritual self-discipline. It seemed a useful subject that would help her to remember to keep her eyes on the sidewalk while she was out walking.

Toward the end of the workshop the moderator led the attendees through a spiritual exercise using an imaginative technique. "Shut your eyes and go into contemplation," he instructed the group. "Two ECK Masters are going to escort you to the Mahanta. The Inner Master is waiting for you." Their assignment was to ask the Mahanta about spiritual self-discipline in their own lives.

Closing her eyes, the woman visualized the two ECK Masters coming for her. Suddenly her focus changed. Instead of visualizing, she was now actually in the inner scene, being escorted by two ECK Masters to a room that was glowing with a warm light.

"Go in, please," they instructed. Inside was the Mahanta, surrounded by a glittering array of material treasures.

"Please sit down," he said, pointing to the chair in front of him. She felt his eyes on her as she sat down and looked around in awe at all the sparkling treasures. She was reminded of the constant urge she'd had lately to go to flea markets and auctions, searching for that one precious object she felt sure was somewhere in the world just waiting for her to discover it.

"The treasures you seek are not of this world," the Mahanta said. Suddenly the shining treasures around them lost their glow and slowly faded away. The Mahanta then reached inside her and pulled out a glowing ball of light and held it in front of her. "You don't need those treasures," he said, "because you already have the golden heart." He then placed the glowing ball back inside of her.

Off in the distance she heard the moderator calling for the people in the workshop to end their contemplation. "It's time for you to go back," the Mahanta said.

She opened her eyes to hear the woman next to her saying, "Well, how did it go?"

"It went fine," she said at first. Then came the conflict: "But I forgot to ask the Master about self-discipline."

She was given an experience that anyone in the room would have traded all their treasures for, yet all she thought about was that she had forgotten to follow the instructions of the moderator and ask the Inner Master about self-discipline. She didn't yet realize that she had gotten far more than she went looking for.

Sometimes it takes a while for the meaning of an experience to sink in. Whether it takes place on the inner planes or out here, often such an experience seems so natural and commonplace that it's easily forgotten or taken for granted.

What Is a Co-worker?

The idea that we are really here to learn to become a Co-worker with God sounds dull to many people. "You're saying that's why I'm here? Don't call me, I'll call you," they say. But many Higher Initiates who are able to work consciously on the inner planes find it a service of great joy.

Being a Co-worker doesn't mean you hear the Voice of God talking to you as you're serving on the inner planes. It's more a matter of realizing that something at that moment needs doing; you are the one most qualified to do it, so you do it. The people around you, on the inner planes even as here, are often unaware of what you are doing or of the service you are giving. The joy comes from loving God; and because you love God, you don't have to take credit for the little things that you do.

Sometimes I'm tempted to try to describe what the other worlds are like; but an esoteric state really can't be explained. If you try to talk about a place you can't explain, most people will say, "That doesn't sound so great." That's simply because they don't know firsthand the inner consciousness and feelings that accompany this experience of God. There is no way you can tell them.

When We Really Let Go

One way they can learn of it is to see in you an example of something they would like to become. They may not know what you have, but they like you. They may not be able to see the Light around you, but they can feel something warm and good. Like the postal clerk who said, "This could be the time to do my good deed for the day." Without realizing it they are responding to the ECK. They are responding to you as a channel for the ECK.

When we really let go, the ECK can work through us very easily. When It does, people respond and are able to receive the help that is coming to them.

As I walk down the street observing people, sometimes I marvel at the infinite combinations of the basic form that makes up the human body. With so many millions of beings made up of a head, a body, two arms and two legs, you would think we'd see duplicates of each other all the time. Yet you have to look pretty hard to find two people who look alike. We're tall, short, light, heavy, with various amounts of hair ranging in color from black to white. Some of us walk sprightly while others have been damaged in some way through the career of experiences in this lifetime. And that doesn't even begin to take into account the experiences of previous lifetimes, all of which have shaped each of us so uniquely.

After a while, anyone who becomes skilled in spiritual psychology can recognize certain types of people. You begin to see certain levels of Soul consciousness shining through, despite the covering of the human body. Eventually you can spot the kind of look that tells you, Watch out. Keep your hand on your wallet; smile, but don't sign anything. Or you can look at other people and know that their heart is as good as the day is long; you can trust them with your life.

River Run to God

Within the first year of studying the ECK discourses, you will have the First Initiation. This initiation takes place in the dream state. Because each one of you is a unique individual, each person's initiation experience is different. Some of the ECKists remember the dream initiation, and some don't.

An individual had an experience on the inner planes which she later determined was her First Initiation. She awoke in the dream state to find herself standing on the bank of a churning body of water that reminded her of the Colorado River. Swift currents disappeared through the canyons. Since you couldn't tell what was around the bend, there was always the danger of rapids or rocks downstream.

Next to her was a raft. She picked up a pole and stepped onto the logs. With great apprehension, she poled the raft off the stones and into the shallows just outside the main current. Just as she was steeling herself to push off into the current, the Mahanta, the Inner Master came along.

"What are you doing?" he called.

"I'm going down the river," she said.

"Would you care for some help?" he offered.

"Sure," she answered gratefully.

For a brief moment he gazed intently into her eyes. "Do you really want help?" he asked again.

"Yes," she answered, "I really want help."

"All right," the Mahanta said. "If you really want help, we'll build you a house on the raft."

She looked at him in surprise. "A house? But won't the raft tip over?"

"No," he said, "The house will give it ballast."

Only later did it occur to her that she didn't even know the meaning of the word *ballast;* it was entirely outside of her normal vocabulary. When she looked it up in a dictionary, she found that one of the definitions stated, "that which gives stability in character."

"OK," she said, "But I don't know how to build a house."

"Don't worry, I'll help," he assured her.

The Master went off to gather some lumber and stacked it near the raft. "I'll cut it to size and show you how to put it in place," he said. "You can use the hammer and nails to fasten the boards."

Floor-by-floor, room-by-room, and wall-by-wall, together they worked to build a house on the raft. Not once during the construction did the Inner Master criticize her for going too slow. At all times she had the freedom to work at her own pace.

Finally the work was finished. "Now you have a house on the raft," the Master said. "Let's go." And they climbed on board.

All at once she knew what the experience meant. Whenever she was ready to go down the river—the unknown journey home to God—the Master would always be there to help her around the blind bends. No matter what was ahead, she would never be alone.

As the woman began her study of the ECK discourses, she was taking the first step in the inner worlds, too. Because she had taken the first step, the Master came to tell her what was needed next: to build a house on the raft. This house represented the knowledge of ECK that she needed in order to survive on the river run to God.

The conflict she had to face was her fear of taking the journey home to God by herself. It was resolved when she was given an experience that showed her what the Master means when he says, "I am always with you." She could now embark on her journey knowing that when trouble came, the Mahanta would always be there to help.

Spiritual Reunion

The hospice program provides help to terminally ill people. A volunteer visits and tries to help the patient feel more comfortable. An ECK initiate had made various attempts to participate in such a program, but for one reason or another his efforts kept being put off. When all the circumstances were right, the Mahanta, the Inner Master, arranged a way for this young man to get started in the program through a personal experience.

One day he got an unexpected urge to go back home to visit relatives he hadn't seen in ten years. One of his first stops was to see his grandfather. At ninety-nine years of age, the old man was deaf and blind. Though his grandfather could still talk, there really was no way to communicate with him; but as soon as the young man touched his hand, the old man began to cry. He recognized his grandson immediately.

During their meeting, the old man told his grandson that he had known him back in San Francisco about sixty years ago. In those days, the grandfather recalled, the younger man had been a carpenter. That didn't seem unlikely to the grandson; in this lifetime he had tried carpentry for a year, but gave it up.

The grandfather was so very happy to be with his grandson again. Just before their meeting was over, he told the younger man that he now felt ready to go. Their reunion had been the only thing he had been waiting for. The grandson realized that what the old man had actually waited for was someone who was a channel for the ECK.

Journeys to the Other Worlds

Soon after this on the inner planes, the Mahanta took the ECKist and his grandfather on a journey to the area where the older man would make his home after he left the physical body.

These journeys to the other worlds are quite common for elderly people. As the time of translation nears, one guide or another comes to help them become familiar with their new home. In this case it was the Mahanta, who at the same time was showing the ECK initiate how to help people over to the other side.

This is one of the services that can be performed by some of those who advance further in ECK. Helping a loved one across to the other side is one of the most enjoyable tasks. The transition to their new home, which is far better than anything here, is very natural.

As part of the initiate's training, the Mahanta cautioned him, "When you bring people over, do not bring them into the Light too fast." The physical world is a world of darkness, really. It may not seem so while we are here, with all the bright lights and sunshine. But by comparison, even the next plane, the Astral Plane, is a world of extreme brilliance.

Because of the bond of love they shared, the grandson was allowed to accompany his grandfather back and forth across the illusory borders of life and death. Night after night, the ECKist's grandfather was gradually introduced to his future home. When the time came for him to move in, he was familiar with it.

Life and death really have no borders; it's all part of the continuum of life. In ECK we learn how to operate, live, and have our being in the continuum of life; to move back and forth at will.

The initiate finally lets go and surrenders to the ECK. By giving up the smaller portion of himself—the ego, the little self—he is able to operate in the full consciousness of Soul. Great things can now be accomplished through him.

Tonight, go within and say to the Inner Master, whoever you envision that to be, "Take me wherever you see fit for my spiritual unfoldment. I go with thee in love."

May the blessings be.

Hawaiian Regional Seminar, Honolulu, Hawaii,
Saturday, November 8, 1986

Cultural shock occurs in spiritual growth, too. We get used to a certain state of consciousness that is comfortable, then the next initiation comes along and takes us to a strange, unknown place.

5

So What Do I Do Now?

How does an ECKist handle situations that arise in his or her life? Sometimes you have to face the lion, because there is no reason to run from it. This is just one of the phases a person goes through.

Just before I got the position of Living ECK Master, I became very ill. One of the things I did to help myself get through it was to join the ECKANKAR Office softball team.

I used to have a strong throwing arm, but by that point my entire body had taken quite a beating. Volunteering for second base, I found I had barely enough strength to throw the ball to first. So I developed a smooth double-play throw from second base over to first, simply because I had to; I didn't have as much time as someone with a stronger arm.

Rewinning Heaven Every Day

Heaven must be rewon every day. No matter what your initiation, the vibrations change every time you reach a new level of consciousness. At first you just don't quite fit in. All your ideas, emotions, and habits are still tied into the level you just came from. You have to adjust in much the same way a longtime resident of Hawaii who suddenly gets transferred to Minneapolis would.

Culture shock occurs in spiritual growth, too. We get used to a certain state of consciousness that is comfortable, then the next initiation comes along and takes us to a strange, unknown place. It's as if the wind suddenly blew in from the northwest with a chill factor of minus fifty-five.

The next step is to figure out as quickly as possible what the natives do to survive. In the spiritual life, it also helps to observe what those at the higher levels of initiation do to survive under conditions of increased Light and Sound. Other ways you can learn are by trial and error or by insight and inspiration, which is better.

Taking Constructive Steps

An initiate who ran into a health situation came to me several times for consultation. Each time she would ask, "Is there something I should know?" It was as if she wanted me to tell her, "Yes, it looks pretty bleak; it's the end of the road for you." Generally I would just suggest that she keep on doing her spiritual exercises, and then I'd ask about her nutrition plan. At the end of our talk, she would leave without the expected assurance that it was her last year on earth.

Recently, she talked again about her health problems and again asked, "Is there something I should know?" I changed the subject, and for a few minutes we spoke about a number of other things. Finally she began to show an interest in how nutrition might play a role in remedying her condition over a period of time. Now she is at the point of taking constructive steps to turn her health around.

72

A Better Way to Live

The further you go in life, in ECK, the more the worlds should open up for you. And they do—on the inner planes. Out here it seems the road narrows: more people seem to be lying in ambush, and if an obstacle can occur, it will.

Sometimes we get frustrated at the wrong things. If we were concerned only with big problems, it would be simpler. We would only have one or two things to worry about. But hundreds of little problems plague us throughout life, and it's the little things that gnaw. For this reason, many people would rather hear about love, survival on earth, and how to make it through to tomorrow.

Even when someone doesn't like this life, they believe it beats going into the vast unknown, no matter how great it's supposed to be. So with each talk I prepare, I face a dilemma. While knowing that your motivation is to find a better way to live here, my purpose is to tell you that this place really isn't so great and that there are other worlds—the high invisible planes of God—where every Soul should yearn to go.

I know you would rather relax than go out and do great spiritual things, because that's how things are; you and I both recognize it. But at least put one-fifth of your attention higher than this earthly existence. You can keep the other four-fifths here, do as well as you can, and be as happy as you can.

Jury Duty

Occasionally initiates tell me about ways the ECK has come in to help them in their everyday life.

A Higher Initiate in Texas was called for jury duty. The trial involved a crime that could involve capital punishment if the defendant were found guilty. In the jury-selection process, she was interviewed by the defendant's attorney, a lawyer from the district attorney's office, and the judge.

The lawyer from the district attorney's office was young and ambitious; this job was merely a stepping-stone to bigger and better things. Prosecuting this case successfully would be good for his career. Since a guilty verdict meant the defendant might have to pay with his life, the lawyer wanted to make sure that religious beliefs wouldn't influence the potential jurors' decisions.

"What religion do you belong to?" he asked the Higher Initiate.

"ECKANKAR," she replied.

This presented an unknown factor to the young attorney. Never having heard of it before, he was suspicious.

"Who's your spiritual leader?" he asked.

"He's called the Living ECK Master," she answered.

During the next two and a half hours of questioning, she had to try to explain the teachings of ECKANKAR to the attorneys and the judge, a woman in her forties.

Finally the lawyer from the district attorney's office asked her outright: "When the time comes to make a decision, how do you think you would vote?"

"I'll let the facts speak for themselves," she said.

That wasn't good enough for him. He repeated the question, more forcefully this time. She gave the same answer as before.

The lawyer looked perplexed. Not knowing otherwise, he equated the Living ECK Master to the Pope, having the same skepticism that many people did back in the days when John F. Kennedy was running for president. Since the United States had never had a Roman Catholic president before, they wondered if this man's decisions would be influenced by the church in Rome rather than the needs of the American people. It became quite an issue.

The lawyer tried again. "When you are locked in the jurors' room and it is time to make a decision, how are you going to vote?" But this time he added, "Does this Living ECK Master teach that you should not take a life?"

The ECKist was getting exasperated by now. In the tone one would use in responding to a persistent child who can't take no for an answer, she said, "I've told you twice before exactly how I am going to make the decision: I will let the facts speak for themselves. What more do you expect me to say?"

With that the ECK initiate turned the tables. No longer meek and intimidated, she took charge. She tried to convey that her religion had not made her biased toward any of the different aspects of life; it had made her objective. But her answers didn't provide the reassurance the attorney sought, so she was rejected as a juror. She didn't mind. She had no interest in having to make a decision that concerned a person's life, yet she had been willing to if that was where the ECK led her.

As she left the room, the judge looked at her and said, "You're quite some woman." The judge obviously respected her for standing up for herself, and mostly for being an individual.

Some of you will run into similar situations. When we are called for jury duty, we have to do our service. This is one of our responsibilities as citizens. This story gives an example of how one initiate handled it. She was a wonderful spokesman for ECK because she expressed what she knew from her point of view and did it in a reasonable way.

Karmic Chain Reaction

A singer and her accompanist got together at the vocalist's home to rehearse a song that they were going to perform at an ECK seminar. The accompanist brought her nine-year-old daughter. The little girl was delighted to find that the host had a pet, a frisky German shepherd. While the two women practiced their number, the girl and the dog went outside to play.

Everything was fine until the dog bumped into some cactus and got a sharp thorn in his paw. Whimpering, he limped over to the girl, his eyes imploring her to pull this painful thing from his paw. Her heart went out to the poor wounded animal; she really wanted to help.

She carefully grasped the end of the thorn and pulled it out. The dog was so happy that he jumped up to lick her face in gratitude, but the energetic force of his weight knocked her backward against the cactus.

The girl cried out sharply then stared in horror at the thorn lodged in her hand. Sizing up the problem, the dog tried to help. He began to swipe at her hand with his paw, attempting to brush the thorn away. The girl screamed and wailed in terror. She thought the animal was attacking her.

The dog began to nudge her toward the house. Crying, the little girl resisted at first, but the dog managed to push her into the house, where her mother was able to take care of the problem.

Sometimes when we help someone, as the girl did, they are so grateful—or in other cases so ungrateful—that our act of kindness turns back on us. Then the karmic chain reaction begins. We find ourselves getting hurt in return, and for a while everything goes crazy. Eventually there is nothing left to do but turn it over to an adult, which in ECK would be the Mahanta. Then the situation is on the way to being made harmonious. In the process, something has been worked off. In this story, both the girl and the dog were able to give love to each other.

Function of Karma

The function of karma is to give us an opportunity to learn to serve God. Many people don't want to hear this: to them, service means having to do something against their will. Yet once a karmic situation has passed and our services are no longer needed, we can go on to another avenue of life and serve again in another way. This allows us not only to pay off a debt to the past but to learn service while doing so.

We may not like to look at it like this, but I think it's healthier to have an understanding of why we are here. Without these reasons our life would seem useless. We would live for nothing but to work, feed our body, and surround ourselves with comfortable props.

Without love, it's all empty — a hollow home in a hollow world. This is why the fountain of love must somehow be opened up within us. Often it is only after a great deal of suffering that the heart is opened up to love.

Essentially there are two kinds of people in the world: those who have love, and those who don't. Many people think they have it, but they don't. And until they know the real meaning of love, they are like the tone-deaf musician, merely going through the motions.

Tone-deaf Musician

I once had a friend who liked to play the piano but was tone-deaf. The man would spread out his sheet music and plunk away at the keys, mechanically following whatever was on the paper in front of him. But because he couldn't distinguish between the notes, the music lacked heart.

You can tell when a musician plays from the heart with love. Somewhere, at some time, something within him has opened up to allow this unexplainable love to come through the door. Once the door is opened, whether very wide or just a little bit, love will always come through to some degree.

This love coming through is what makes life worth living. If you have it, you know what I'm talking about. If you don't have it, you probably think I'm just speaking philosophically. People who have love are compassionate; they can understand the plight of others very easily. Those who don't have it are harsh and critical, always looking for the worst in others. Those who have love always look for the best.

Cycles of Life

In ancient Egypt, in the time of Pythagoras, there was a man called Polycrates. He was the tyrant of Samos, a small island located in the Aegean Sea just off the mainland of Turkey. Polycrates took over the island and subjugated the people, but at the same time he began to construct splendid buildings and recreate the culture, bringing Samos to political and commercial preeminence.

Polycrates was known as a very fortunate man who was blessed by the gods in all ways. His friend and ally, a very wise Egyptian pharaoh, once tried to explain to him that life has its ups and downs, that an up cycle must always be attended by a down cycle. This is the nature of life, the pharaoh said, the balance which always occurs. It is part of the rhythm of living.

Polycrates merely laughed. To prove his ongoing favor with the gods, he removed an expensive ring from his finger and threw it in the sea. Then he calmly turned and walked away.

The next day a fisherman came to the castle clutching the ring in his hand. "I found this ring in the belly of a fish I caught this morning," he explained to the guardians of the gate. "It is obviously a royal ring. I would like to return it." The palace officials rewarded him handsomely and brought the ring to the tyrant.

Polycrates took one look at the ring and burst into laughter. To him the whole thing was a hilarious joke that proved once again his favor with the gods. He actually believed that if you had enough wealth and influence, only good things could happen to you in life. He was wrong, of course, because his consciousness was in an almost infantile stage of development.

When the Egyptian heard of this incident, he immediately informed his close advisers that he was severing his alliance with the Greek. "That much fortune is bound to bring the displeasure of the gods," he said. The Egyptian, having seen more of life through the teachings of his own culture, knew that what goes up must come down.

The ancient Egyptians were far ahead of the Greeks. The secrets and mysteries of the initiation rites that later developed in the Greek mystery schools—by Pythagoras, for instance—were all borrowed from the Egyptians and modified to fit the Greek mind.

In ECK we realize that whatever we face—the good karma as well as the bad, the up wave and the down wave—is here only to make us a more experienced Soul who will one day become a full Co-worker with God. Even now, we are each functioning in varying degrees as a Co-worker with God, imperfect but in the process of becoming more perfect. The only way this can occur is through experience. We are here on earth only to glean and gather the experiences of life in whatever circumstances life has placed us—through our job, family, hobbies, physique, illnesses, and so on.

The Prodigal Son

No matter what we are faced with, Soul must eventually come to the point where It says, "I know there is a way. I may not know at this moment what it is, but there is always a way." When this surrender to the Mahanta occurs, the door will open wider, allowing enough love in to let you meet the obstacle or challenge at hand. It will always do this. But being aware of it and being able to accept it depends on the individual's ability to surrender to this principle of life—to the Holy Spirit, the ECK. In so doing, you rise to the pinnacle of the spiritual worlds and enter the kingdom of heaven.

Most of you are familiar with the biblical story of the prodigal son. It goes something like this.

One day the younger of two sons approached his wealthy father. "All I do every day is work, work, work," he griped. "I want to go out and have a good time. I want something better out of life. Father, I would like to have my inheritance now."

"Why?" his father asked.

"Because I'm young and I want to live."

"All right," his father agreed. "I'll divide my wealth between you and your brother, and I wish you well on your journey." So the young man packed his belongings and left home to go out into the world.

For a time everything went well. The wasteful son went to a lot of wild parties and made plenty of friends, his popularity lasting as long as he was able to pick up the tab. But just about the time his money ran out, famine and drought swept over the land. Times got so hard that he couldn't even buy food. Finally, in desperation, he hired himself out on a farm.

"You want a job, you can take care of my pigs out there in the field," the farmer said. "Take their food to them every day." The young man was so hungry that he was happy to eat the husks that were fed to the pigs.

One day he woke up and came to his senses. Here I am taking care of the pigs, he thought, lucky to be eating the same food they do. Back at my father's house, even the servants live better than this. I'm going back home. I'll ask my father to hire me as a servant. Even a job as a humble servant is better than being a swineherd.

So he began his journey back home.

While he was still a distance away, his father, who watched the road daily in the hope that his son would one day return, saw him coming. He ran out to greet him.

Before the young man had a chance to tell his father that he wanted a job as one of his servants, the father pulled him into the house. Seeing his son's humble condition, he gave him a new robe, a ring, and even shoes for his feet. "Now let's have a feast!" his father said.

The older brother heard the sounds of merrymaking as he came in from working in the fields. "What's going on?" he asked one of the servants. "It sounds like a party."

"It is a party," the servant said. "Your brother came home."

"But why have a party for that?" the brother said.

"Your brother was really in a shambles," the servant said. "But your father fixed him up. He's so happy to have him back that he's throwing a feast."

The older brother was bitter. "I'm the one who has been faithful," he complained to his father. "I stayed home. I worked and sweated for you every day. Why should my brother get all this?"

"Because he who was dead has come back and is alive," his father said. "Let's rejoice for that."

We never find out whether the older brother was able to accept this.

Ability to Love

Soul goes into the lower worlds as the prodigal son. There are other Souls, the inexperienced sons, who stay home and continue to live the good life. In this story, the prodigal son's years of experience on the road taught him more than his brother. The one who remained at home was essentially serving himself and those in his immediate vicinity.

Even though the older son stayed home to work for his father, somehow life had not taught him how to love. And because he didn't have love, he resented his brother. The one who left and then returned home now knew the meaning of love and gratitude, a gift he earned through immense suffering.

Occasionally someone comes to me in great distress over a mismatch in a relationship, where one person loves and the other does not. "What can I do?" the individual asks. "I love this person but he (or she) doesn't love me."

I can only suggest that maybe one person has had more experiences that have opened the heart to love, whereas the other person has not. In that case, you are better off to look for someone who can reciprocate the love.

The answer is that simple, yet it's very difficult to do, because we are too close to the situation to see which way is out. It's easier to be like the son who safely stayed home.

Rebellion against the Law

A certain Higher Initiate had always rebelled against man-made laws. Once he became an initiate, and especially a Higher Initiate, he felt he should no longer have to be bound by human laws. Consequently, he was often in trouble for things such as speeding violations and not paying his taxes.

His constant rebellion led to confrontations with angry police officers and hassles in court. Nobody was interested in his reasons for breaking the laws. All the police and judges really cared about was whether or not he was guilty of going above the speed limit. If so, just pay the fine. Any attempts to argue about it only made things worse for him.

One day he realized that his constant fighting against man-made laws was making him very unhappy. His attitude had accomplished nothing. It was just causing him a lot of trouble. Was it possible he might be doing something wrong? As he thought it over, it occurred to him that the ECK Masters made it a point to observe the man-made laws. But why? he wondered.

He began to consider the benefits of obeying laws. For one thing, he thought, breaking them made the law enforcers very angry. For another, it only made more karma for him. That was a start: Fear of karma as expressed through the judicial system was a valid reason for observing the laws. Yet he realized he still hadn't gotten to the heart of the matter.

Soon after that the answer came to him in contemplation. The answer was simply, Love is all.

Finally he started to understand why the ECK Masters obeyed the man-made laws. The Masters recognize that, here on earth, the people who make the laws do the best they can to maintain an orderly society where violence doesn't run rampant, where there is some redress for injuries and wrongdoing. The system may not be perfect, but that's because it's designed by imperfect people in an imperfect world. The ECK Masters obey the man-made laws because of their great love for those in the human state of consciousness.

Love Is All

The Higher Initiate asked for further insight into the answer he had gotten.

Still in contemplation, he was taken to a temple at Honardi, a retreat for ECK Masters on the Soul Plane. Escorting him were Gopal Das, Rebazar Tarzs, and Wah Z. In the library of the temple, encased in glass, he saw a small holographic version of the twelve books of the Shariyat-Ki-Sugmad.

As he came closer, the seventh book emerged from the casing and floated over to a projector. The pages quickly fanned forward, then came to a stop. Words began to flash against a screen, explaining to the initiate the meaning of the saying, *Love is all.*

When he returned to the body, he realized he had a new understanding of the power of love to conquer all. He now knew why, if one operated and worked with the spirit of love, life became much easier for him. The spirit of love brings compassion and understanding. To be without it is to be critical, always finding fault with others, and always worried about other people's motives rather than your own.

We all drift in and out of this state of love. None of us is purely in the state of love or no love; it's just that each person is generally more in one state than the other.

The door of love is open for all in ECK, but for some it's open wider and more often. The only difference is in the degree. The ECK initiations are meant to open this door more and more—so that we can see the reasons for our own experiences with a spiritual perspective; so that we can look with compassion at the experiences of others and say, "There but for the grace of God go I." The Spiritual Exercises of ECK open this door to the Holy Spirit, which truly is all we have.

True Surrender

I would like to read a short poem. Though stated in more conventional terms, to the ECKist it speaks of surrender to the Mahanta. The poet is someone you all know well, a writer prolific on any subject, in every field of human endeavor, whether it be philosophy, religion, metaphysics, or the humanities. The poet's name is Anonymous.

> As children bring their broken toys with tears
>   for us to mend,
> I brought my broken dreams to God, because
>   He was my friend.
> But then instead of leaving Him in peace to
>   work alone,
> I hung around and tried to help with ways that
>   were my own.
> At last I snatched them back and cried,
>   "How can you be so slow?"
>
> "My child," He said, "what could I do?
>   You never did let go."

Look for the ECK in the face of all you meet, for then you will see the face of the Mahanta, the face of love. Love is what opens all doors for you, everywhere, in all the worlds.

Hawaiian Regional Seminar, Honolulu, Hawaii,
November 9, 1986

Over and over the thought kept running through his
mind: If I had waited only five seconds more.

6

Only Five Seconds More

The purpose of ECK seminars is to tell people about ECK, the Light and Sound, Soul Travel, and all the different aspects of the Holy Spirit. This information is useful to anyone who wants to make this life a little bit easier to live and who wants to take the most direct route home to God.

Situations that Slow Us Down

Several of us were checking in for the flight to Melbourne. There were quite a few lines at the ticket counter. My wife and two friends tried to figure out which line was moving the fastest. "I guess it really doesn't matter," my wife said. "Whichever one we take is going to slow down."

Those who serve the ECK may have noticed that if there is a way to make things more difficult, that way will be found. Especially before ECK seminars, routine tasks that normally go very quickly and easily become a little bit harder and take longer to accomplish. It seems to be an unwritten rule.

It isn't that we look for trouble by acknowledging these things; it's simply a matter of fact. You can only go so long having nice thoughts about how smoothly everything is going to run, but then you find out otherwise. Finally you just accept the way it is and do the best you can to get through it.

They chose a line where the ticket clerk happened to be training a new person. The lines on both sides were moving ahead steadily, but ours was practically at a standstill. Just as we got to the ticket counter, the trainer and trainee were replaced by a clerk who reminded me of Battle-Ax Annie. She immediately began to rattle off a list of reasons, rules, and regulations about the size and weight of our baggage being too much to carry on the plane. We would have to check it and like it.

Last year we noticed that international airlines were cutting back on the number of bags you could carry on board. This year my wife and I had carefully packed one small bag each. This way, we figured, we could take whatever we needed on the plane with us, and not have to spend time collecting our luggage at the baggage-claim area when we landed. Nevertheless, the woman behind the counter insisted that we had to check our bags. Since there was nothing we could do about it, we agreed. Luckily I had a paperback book in hand, so I had reading material for the flight.

As we boarded the plane, I noticed that most of the people who had gotten on before us had all kinds of extra baggage with them. They must have been in one of the other lines. Anyone our clerk had checked was lucky to carry a handkerchief on board.

Unwanted Garbage

We had made very specific arrangements through our travel agent, and again at the ticket counter, to be seated in the nonsmoking section. Our ticket clerk had seemed very obliging on that point, but the seats she had assigned us were in the smoking section.

When one of the flight attendants came by, we asked if we could move to the nonsmoking section. He very kindly offered to see if any seats were available. A few minutes later he came back. "There's a whole row of seats in the back of the plane that the flight attendants use," he said. "Since this is a short flight, we'll be very busy. You're welcome to use them."

We walked to the back of the plane, smiling triumphantly. How good we felt! No matter that Battle-Ax Annie back at the airport had done her best to make our trip miserable; other people on this airline were trying to make us comfortable.

As soon as we sat down, I detected a strong odor of garbage. On the floor near our feet we noticed two huge orange bags, the kind that clean-up crews use along the highways. The smile quickly left my face. Were garbage fumes better or worse than smoke?

After a while the smell grew stronger and more offensive. I kicked at the bag, trying to move it farther away. One of the flight attendants looked over at us very sternly, then glanced down at the orange bags. No doubt he was concerned that one of us would accidentally knock the bag open—which is exactly what I did with my second kick. We thought the flight would never end.

Outer Reflections of Consciousness

I often walk the streets in cities we visit, pondering new ways to present the teachings of ECK. ECK is the Holy Spirit, which is the Light and Sound of God. Basically the ECK teachings show you how to make contact with these two aspects of the divine consciousness. At many of the seminars I give spiritual exercises which people can try in the privacy of their own homes, if they are willing. This helps them find out for themselves if the teachings of ECK are for them.

I walk along the streets trying to get a feel for the consciousness of the people in an area. Changes in food preferences, dress styles, and other outer patterns may seem of no consequence to others, but to me they reflect a change in consciousness.

The outer circumstances also make a very definite impression on the inner life. In New Zealand, for instance, the government recently imposed a 10 percent goods-and-services tax on food, clothing, even medicine. Many people thought times were so hard before the tax that they could barely make it, and now they have to come up with 10 percent more. So they are finding that they have to do things differently than before—shop more carefully, take less time off for recreation, and so on. They have to scrimp in every area.

When Karma Speeds Up

The karmic pattern of their country is speeding up, as it is in other parts of the world. People begin to feel the effects of the ECK, the Holy Spirit, the wind of change. At the same time, the karma of the individuals in that area is also speeding up. There is a direct connection between national and individual karma. When it speeds up in the macrocosm, it will also speed up in the micro-cosm, and vice versa.

Most of us resist change because we don't really like it. Given a choice, we would choose to keep our lives comfortable. But unfortunately in the human state of consciousness, one doesn't learn as well when everything is going his way. Soul becomes selfish and self-serving, with no interest in serving others. It loses sight of the mission for which It came here—to become a Co-worker with God. Not to become one with God or any of those passive notions, but to become a Co-worker with God.

In ECK we live an active life. We may not know what tomorrow will bring, but it doesn't matter; we try to do the best we can today with the spiritual insight that we have gained through the Spiritual Exercises of ECK.

Glimpses of the Past

Sometimes we have experiences along the Time Track which enable us to see our past lives—if this is what we really want. And sometimes when we get what we asked for, we find it is not really what we want.

An initiate mentioned that before he came to ECK, he wanted to see his past lives so badly that he tried in every way he could to read the Akashic records. Then he found ECK, and he diligently applied the spiritual exercises toward that goal. As the Holy Spirit began to open him up, he started to get glimpses of his past lives.

But it didn't happen only during contemplation or in his dreams; it got to the point where he would see Roman soldiers marching by even when he was fully awake or trying to work. He was given so many experiences of the past that he actually began to beg the Inner Master, the Mahanta, to close off this particular ability. He had no more need of it; he'd had his fill of past lives. Now he does the spiritual exercises to gain insight into his daily life and to help him to meet the problems of everyday existence.

Moving On

Most people are motivated to stay here on earth for as long as possible. Yet my motive is to point out that, in one way or another, life on earth will one day be forfeited. When the time is up, each individual will have to go. It's that simple.

In ECK we learn what the other worlds are like. Though we recognize that we do what we can for survival while we're here, when the time comes to take the step from this world to the next, we are not afraid. It's a very gentle, quick, and easy step.

I mentioned this to an audience in Hawaii: while they were looking for ways to stay here, I was trying to tell them what it's like to leave here. Somehow we were viewing the situation from different ends. A gentleman in the audience, perhaps eighty years old, suddenly started laughing out loud. He thought the whole idea—that the longer you stay here, the better it looks—was uproariously funny. But he was an ECKist; he didn't have any fear of the process of translation, which is usually called death.

Figuring Things Out

ECK is actually the path of life. We want to know what to do with our life to make it worth the trouble. What makes this life meaningful? Why is today more meaningful than yesterday? What is the purpose of all the little things that occur?

Sometimes the answer is easy. If hot oil splashes on us while we're cooking at the stove, we can be pretty sure it happened because we were careless. But other things aren't so easy to figure out.

For instance, if an individual you work with is angry at you day after day, you naturally wonder why. Sometimes the Inner Master will open up a past life just enough for you to see where the karmic problem with this person was created. With this insight, you can figure out what must be done so that you will no longer be tied to him like a convict to a prison post. Then the chain can be released, and you can move as far away from this individual as you like.

Karma binds us to the people around us, to our homes, and to our jobs. We can try to run away from karma, from responsibility for our actions; but somewhere along the way, the day will come when we have to face ourselves. The teachings of ECK give us the courage and the know-how to face ourselves in this lifetime and to do it as well as we can.

Unexpected Assistance at the Mall

On my last trip to Melbourne, I walked past a rock group performing at the shopping mall. The music was so loud that it hurt my ears. The lead singer made more of a racket with his voice and discordant guitar than the rest of the band put together.

There were many people milling about, and it was taking a while to get past them. Finally I couldn't take it any longer. I started to turn away. Whatever the ECK wills, so be it, I thought. I just wanted to get out of there.

As I worked my way through the crowd, I turned and glanced back toward the band. A bizarre scene met my eyes. The lead singer was moving backward down the mall, so fast it looked as if he were competing in a strange kind of footrace. He kept right on going until he fell, landing flat on his back in the middle of the mall. The rest of the band just kept playing—they were so caught up in their music that they never missed him.

A few people from the crowd ran over to him. Pretty soon the other band members realized their singer had stopped, so they looked around to see what had happened. And there he was, stretched out on the floor, flat on his back. A couple of the onlookers helped him to his feet and held him as he hobbled shakily to one of the benches off to the side.

Sometimes when life seems too heavy, when the noise level gets to the point where you can't take another minute of whatever the negative powers are throwing at you, something happens to help you. All you can say about it is, "May the blessings be," and leave no bad feelings behind. But I was certainly glad he had stopped that awful singing. And no, I was not the one who caused it. This is the path of love, not fear.

Psychic Dabblers

As people begin moving toward the spiritual path of ECK, they often dabble in psychic areas. The psychic fields are generally concerned with how to be happy by gaining power over others. The people who dabble in these areas like to find some way to impress upon you how powerful they are in controlling your life.

Unfortunately, many people are naive. They don't recognize that such a person has no more influence, knowledge, or power than a sparrow chirping in the street during a rainstorm. Did the sparrow make the rain? No; you and I know that's ridiculous. Yet some of the psychic dabblers would have you believe that they are vested with the power to make things happen.

One day a man who dabbled in the psychic arts approached an ECKist who had just moved to a better apartment. "I got you that place," he tried to tell her.

"No, you didn't," she said. She was on to him.

"I have my method of knowing that it was I who helped you," he said, hinting at secret powers.

"Oh? How is that?" she asked.

He said, "The day I heard that you moved, I was listening to my radio. I said, 'If I was responsible for her move, then let the radio stop.' And the radio stopped playing. I knew it was true, because this is how the inner voices speak to me, and they can never be wrong."

"You're crazy," the ECKist said. Then she went on to explain, "The power of ECK protects me, and you are invading my psychic space. You can't do that."

When he protested, she said, "If you keep interfering in my life, everything you are throwing at me is going to come back to you. That's how the Law of Cause and Effect rebukes the person who abuses it."

The man hadn't known that before; no one had ever told him. So even though he was not in ECK, an ECKist was able to point out to him the very simple Law of Cause and Effect. Someday he may take it to heart, get off his high horse, and realize that he cannot try to control the lives of people who are on the path to God, any more than he would want others to control his life.

Retaining Personal Freedom

ECK is the path of freedom. We want the spiritual freedom to move about and live our lives without interference from other people. But this means freedom with responsibility. It doesn't mean you can strut into another person's space, tell him how to live his life, then claim you are living the life of ECK. Because if you impose your viewpoint on others without invitation, you are not living the life of ECK. ECK gives people the freedom to be themselves.

The only time you don't give others the freedom to be themselves is when they move out of their own little world and invade your space. If they try to move into areas which are not their domain, then you simply say, "You don't belong here." The ECK path is not made up of people who let others walk all over them. On the other hand, we are not overbearing people who tromp all over others either. To walk the spiritual path of ECK is to take the middle path.

During the dream state or in contemplation, we are sometimes made aware of how we have strayed over the line of someone else's personal freedom. Often our direction is given in a very apparent way by the Inner Master. If we do not catch the lesson the first time, the Inner Master gives us another nudge through a different means.

In one way or another the Mahanta says, "You have crossed the line. Please wake up, because if you keep this up, you are going to run head-on into yourself." And if you still don't recognize what you are doing, you certainly will meet yourself—on your own ground, on equal terms, in the right way, at the right time.

ECK is the path of love, and that includes learning to have compassion and understanding when other people run into karma that they cannot understand or handle. The ECKist is one who offers comfort, a kind word, and perhaps a shoulder to cry on. But when a person's loss is so deep that words won't help, listening sometimes does more good than talking. This is all part of the path of ECK.

A certain individual is very inspiring to people who are interested in the path of ECK. Her life is a shining example of what it means to be an ECKist—to be involved in this world, to be in this world but not of it. But as more and more people in her area began to join ECKANKAR, the local spiritualist groups and psychic groups sat up and took notice: Their own members were leaving and going to ECKANKAR.

One of these groups began to hold special meetings in which they prayed for this woman to please hurry up and die. They wanted her to go on to the other side, enjoy herself there, and get out of their territory.

When the ECKist showed no signs of leaving, they figured they had better try something other than prayer.

One day the head of the psychic group called her on the phone and said, "We are having meetings on your behalf." The man then explained to her exactly what they were doing.

The ECK initiate said, "Don't you know you can't harm me? The protection of the Light and Sound of God surround me at all times. Don't you realize that the evil you are sending my way can only come back to you and harm you?"

The man then let it slip that he and the other prayer-group members had been very sick lately. "You ought to think about that," the ECKist pointed out.

Initiations in ECK History

As we begin the path of ECK by studying the ECK discourses, generally within the first year comes the experience on the inner planes known as the First Initiation, or the Dream Initiation. Here the Mahanta, the Inner Master, meets the individual and gives this inner initiation as a preliminary linkup with the Holy Spirit. The full linkup is given at the Second Initiation, which means when this lifetime has ended, the initiate is no longer compelled to return to the physical world.

The ECK initiations go way back through history. The most historically recent ones on record were borrowed from the ancient Egyptians when Pythagoras, the Greek philosopher, traveled to Egypt. There, after much hardship, he was given instruction in the Egyptian rites. Returning home, he found that the Greeks did not have the level of awareness or the spiritual stamina of the Egyptians; the initiations had to be adjusted to fit the consciousness of his people.

The teachings of ECK are presented to the people of each era in a certain way, just as the ECK initiations are transformed to fit the people of the times. For instance, no longer is the First Initiation given outwardly, as it was in ancient Egypt and later in Greece. A Greek student was required to go to a dark, lonely cave outside of town and stay there overnight. Leading up to it, the initiator or the Master would provoke the student's fears as much as possible. If the individual spent the night in the cave facing his fears, then the karma which had created the fears would be dissolved by the morning sunlight.

Occasionally a student would refuse the initiation, telling the Master, "I don't have to go to that cave to be spiritual." The Master would never insist; he knew the individual didn't want to do it because of his fear.

It was very dangerous to walk the roads at night in those times. You were taking your life in your hands just to get to the place of initiation. A student may have gone halfway down the road to the cave then changed his mind and turned back. Since this was the preliminary initiation, sometimes the Master would relent and give the student a chance to go back to the cave later.

Early Testing

At the time, the Master gave the ECK teachings under the guise of the mystery schools to fit the current conditions. When a new student first came to the group, he was accepted into the outer, social, circle. He would meet with the other initiates for refreshments and conversation. They would bring up certain subjects, invite his arguments, criticize him, and banter back and forth. The purpose was to draw him out, to see what kind of a person he was, to find out about his feelings and thoughts. Their observations were then reported to the Master.

Before the Master made himself known to the individual, he would sometimes join in the conversation in disguise, perhaps chiding or arguing with the person just to see how he would react.

If the new student got through that stage, he would then be given a more strenuous test. Failure meant he would not be allowed into the mystery school in that lifetime; the door was closed to him, period.

The scenario might go like this:

The would-be initiate is having a good time socializing with the other students. Suddenly, without warning, two men come to get him. He is escorted to a cell and given dry bread and water. He is then handed a slate with one of Pythagoras' symbols—perhaps the triangle, circle, square, or cube. "You must work out the meaning of this symbol," they instruct. Clues were given to him in the days he had spent in the mystery school, but if he had been too busy socializing, he probably missed them.

Twelve or fifteen hours later he is taken out of the cell and brought before a court of his peers, young men who are just a little bit ahead of him on the path.

"You have had plenty of time to work on it," they say. "What did you discover about the secret of the symbol?"

He just stands there, staring at the slate. He has nothing to say about it; all he sees is a drawing of a symbol. The others make fun of him, "You've had fifteen hours to think about it. You ought to know by now what the secret is. How do you expect to be admitted into this mystery school? How do you expect to be given the wisdom of the Holy Spirit if you don't apply yourself and develop correct habits?"

The individual tries to offer an explanation, but someone uses clever logic to refute his arguments.

A number of reactions might be displayed by the person on trial. He may become frustrated and throw his slate to the ground, begin to scream back at the hecklers, or call down the wrath of the gods on this group of people who were making fun of him. Or he might get angry and blame the Master, accusing him of not being a true Master.

At this point the Master would step out from behind a curtain and announce, "You are no longer welcome here. Please go; leave this group you have such a low opinion of."

How ECKists Are Today

This was one of the more difficult initial tests the aspirants were given in those days. ECKists today often feel that they are going through very difficult tests—and indeed they are; but they are tests fitted for the conditions and culture of the twentieth century.

We are not required to spend the night in a sepulcher as they did in Egypt, or in a lonely cave as they did in Greece. In those times, such rituals fit the consciousness of the people. An outward test of courage was needed in order to make an impression on them. Without it, they would not feel they were getting any real truth in the mystery school. It was one of the first circles and one of the first doors through which they had to pass.

The path of ECK has evolved since then, and the initiations are not at all fearsome. Today the First Initiation is often given with an experience of Light and Sound. The Master comes to the individual on the inner planes, takes some of the karma from him, and lets him know that he may now go on to the second year of study in ECK. Then, when he has completed the second year of study, he may qualify for the Second Initiation.

During the time of Christ, whether one believes it or not, the people were of a very low consciousness compared to now. Christ was at the Mental Plane eventually, though not at the time. The Mental Plane is what Saint Paul meant when he spoke of having been caught up to the third heaven. Many people today are already operating at the Astral and Causal levels—the first and second planes beyond the physical.

But these are still not the spiritual worlds of the Soul Plane and beyond. This is where I try to direct the individual. To reach Self-Realization and God-Realization, he must aim for the higher area of the spiritual life. The most direct fashion and the most direct line to achieve this is through the Spiritual Exercises of ECK.

Outer Vehicles

Those of you who are ECKists must remember that when you speak the message of ECK to others, it is not you who comes up with whatever is being said; it is the ECK speaking through you. But when you are finished, it is you who leaves, while the ECK stays with the individual.

When I give a talk, at a certain point it just shuts off. I could probably sit here very quietly and not say a word, yet the ECK would still come through. But as long as I'm here, I figure I might as well give you whatever hints I can.

Unfortunately, not many people are unfolded to the level where they can hear the Inner Master give the truth needed to take them further on the journey home to God. It is simply not possible at first. A person in the physical body needs a Master in the physical body. Some may resent hearing this, but that is just the way it is. People are too busy working every day, trying to make a living. They don't have time to sit down in contemplation and find the direction themselves. On their own it would take lifetimes, just as it took lifetimes to come to the point where we are right now.

Initiation Experience

A new ECKist from Australia had been wondering what her First Initiation would be like. When she was ready for it, a Higher Initiate in ECK came to her in the dream state and said, "Come, let us go see the Master." Together the new ECKist and the Higher Initiate journeyed to one of the worlds of the Astral Plane, chatting as they walked along. Soon the Master appeared in the Light body, and the First Initiation was given.

The individual went on to complete her second year of study, at which time she was ready for the Second Initiation. This one is given on the outer and the inner at the same time, and this is where the full linkup with the Holy Spirit occurs.

As she sat with the ECK Initiator in contemplation, she became aware that the initiator was leading her down a beach. The setting was very familiar; she had been there in the dream state many times since childhood. Is this real or am I imagining it? she wondered.

All of a sudden her consciousness was fully on the inner plane. She and the initiator were met by the ECK Master Rebazar Tarzs, who joined them in their walk along the beach.

Ahead of them on the sand was a blanket spread with fruit. The Inner Master, the Mahanta, was waiting for them. In his hands he held a goblet made of precious jewels. "This is the water of life," he said to her. "Take it, and drink."

This water of life is actually the ECK, which is the Light and Sound of God. Once a person drinks of it, he will never be the same. He will always thirst for the waters of heaven. Never again can he walk in this world without the vision of the inner planes, his heart longing to return to the Far Country from which he came.

When the experience was over, the initiate came back to the physical consciousness. She knew then that the outer and the inner initiation of the Second Circle had been completed.

This is the sort of thing that occurs during the ECK initiation. You become aware that ECK is the path of love. When this connection between Soul and the Holy Spirit is made, it is simply to give the person the best opportunity to live his life in the most fruitful way possible. It allows him to make his way home to the Ocean of Love and Mercy, which we call God or SUGMAD, by the most direct route.

All too often on the path of ECK the tests seem to go on and on. Sometimes they last for one, two, or three years, depending upon the individual and the level of initiation. And sometimes we even get to the point where we say, "I just can't wait any longer. I've waited all this time, and all I get are promises that someday something great will happen to me."

Only Five Seconds More

This brings us to the title of this talk, "Only Five Seconds More." My daughter, who enjoys writing stories, is ripe ground for a storyteller. This one was told to her by her algebra teacher.

There once was a man who worked in a bank. All day long he pushed other people's money back and forth through the teller's window. Hour after hour, day after day, year after year, he would take it in or hand it out, until eventually he grew very tired of it.

One day he went to the park and sat on a bench to eat his lunch. A man strolled over, paused for a few seconds, then sat down next to him and struck up a conversation. "You look so unhappy," the stranger said. "What's the matter?"

The bank teller took another bite of his sandwich and looked straight ahead. He really didn't feel much like talking. But after thinking it over, he decided he had nothing to lose by confiding in this man.

"There really is no reason to continue living," he began. "Every day I go to work at the bank, and all I do is handle money. I push it across the counter, people push it at me. But the problem is, none of it is mine." He stared at the ground for a moment before going on: "Frankly, I'm not very happy here on earth."

"Well, there is something you can do about it," the stranger said.

The bank teller looked doubtful.

"You may believe me or not," the man said. "It's up to you."

The bank teller regarded the other man curiously. What was he talking about?

"Go several blocks down this street," the man said,

pointing ahead, "then turn to the right. Just keep walking until you come to the Acme Travel Agency."

The bank teller was listening closely now.

"As soon as you open the door, you will see an elderly man wearing a very old suit. He will be sitting there quietly. Just walk in, wait in the lobby, and soon you will be shown what else to do."

The bank teller finished his lunch and returned to work. Throughout the day he thought about what the stranger had told him. Should he believe it or not?

The next day he made up his mind. Why not just go there? he thought. What do I have to lose? He was so tired of his job and his life.

At lunchtime he left the bank and went back to the park. From there he began to follow the stranger's directions, not really daring to expect anything. But a short time later, there it was—the Acme Travel Agency. He walked the last few steps to the entrance, took a deep breath, then pushed open the door and went inside.

The first person he saw was the elderly gentleman in his wrinkled, well-worn suit. But the old man was busy with other matters; he didn't even glance up.

A receptionist came over to the bank teller. "Can I help you?" she asked politely.

"Yes," he said. "I want to take a trip."

The receptionist directed him to one of the travel agents. The bank teller went over and sat down in the chair next to her desk.

"Where would you like to go?" she asked, smiling pleasantly. "How about Hawaii or the Virgin Islands?"

"I want to go to a place where people are really happy," he answered.

The travel agent reached for a stack of papers and

flipped through it. Pulling out a photograph, she held it up in front of the teller. It was a picture of a group of people smiling gaily for the camera. Everyone looked so happy.

"Yes," he said. "I would like to go there. How much will it cost?"

"The money in your pocket," she answered.

Emptying his pocket, the bank teller came up with $5.23. "I'm afraid this is all I have," he said.

"All right," she said, and held out her hand for the money. He gave it to her readily. What a small price to pay for this trip, he thought.

"Now listen very carefully," she said, handing him a yellow receipt. "There is a bus stop a block from here. But do not go directly to it, because if you do, you will find nothing but an ordinary bus stop. You must first walk around the block six times, and *then* go to the bus stop."

The instructions seemed rather odd, but the bank teller decided to follow them. What the heck, he thought. If it works out, I won't have to go back to work after lunch. If not, what difference will it make?

A light drizzle greeted him as he left the travel agency. He raised his jacket collar up around his neck and completed his six turns around the block as quickly as possible, then went over to the bus stop. The rain was coming down steadily now. A number of unhappy-looking people stood huddled together in a rickety bus shelter that looked like a little shanty. Noticing that they all had yellow travel receipts clutched in their hands, the bank teller quietly joined the group.

Wet and shivering, they waited, impatiently watching the street. After what seemed a very long time, an old jalopy of a bus pulled up in front of them and stopped. The bus driver, who looked like he hadn't had a shave in many days, stuck his head out the door. The teller was further dismayed to see that the man's clothes were shabby and unwashed.

"Anybody who's going to Verna, board here," the driver yelled. The teller checked his ticket, confirmed that it said *Verna*, and reluctantly climbed on the bus with the others.

When the last passenger had boarded, the door quickly slammed shut behind him. The bus sputtered to a start and slowly took off. Soon they were chugging down a long, bumpy road, and for the next several hours the passengers were bounced around and thrown from side to side. After a while it got so hot that they opened the windows, but no breeze found its way inside.

They traveled all through the day. Just as the sky began to darken and the bus had cooled down to a tolerable temperature, the driver braked to a stop. "OK, everybody out," he ordered.

Looking out the window, the bank teller saw nothing but a very old, weatherbeaten barn. "Is this some kind of a joke?" he said.

"You want to go to Verna, don't you?" the bus driver asked.

"That's what I thought, but if this is Verna . . ."

"Make up your mind," the driver said. "Are you staying here or coming back to town?"

The bank teller watched as the other passengers got off the bus and walked to the barn. They tugged open the two big swinging doors and went inside. "Oh, why not," he finally said. "I'm staying." He stepped down from the bus and hurried to catch up with the others.

As soon as he got inside, the rain started again, quickly turning into a heavy downpour. Water dripped down from the leaky roof; the wind crept in through the cracks in the wall. His teeth chattered from the cold. He covered himself with straw, trying to keep warm.

By daybreak he'd had enough. "I can't take this madness even five seconds longer," he said. "I'm getting out of here."

He jumped up and ran for the doors, not slowing down until he got clear of the barn. When he finally stopped and looked back, he saw that the doors were slowly closing behind him. But then he saw something else that completely amazed him: A beautiful bright yellow light shone inside the barn, enfolding the people who remained. Their faces glowed with happiness.

The bank teller knew he had made a mistake.

"Hey, wait," he called out, breaking into a run. "Wait for me!" But just as he reached the barn, the doors swung tightly shut. He pulled and tugged and pried, and at last he got them open and rushed inside.

No one was there. The barn was dark and empty. Cold wind blew in through the cracks, rain spattered down from the roof. The teller just stood there, feeling lost and alone.

A few minutes later, not knowing what else to do, he left the barn and trudged back out to the road. He hadn't gone very far when the old jalopy bus drove up and stopped alongside of him. "Want to go back to town?" the driver yelled out.

"Might as well," the bank teller answered, sighing heavily.

"Where to?" the driver asked.

"Acme Travel Agency," he said. Maybe he could get another ticket.

The bus driver let him off at the door. Inside, the same receptionist greeted him. "Can I help you?" she asked.

"I want to see my travel agent again," he said.

She pointed the way.

The travel agent looked up and saw him standing at

her desk. "You're back," she said. "By the way, you left some money here yesterday. Here it is." Without another word, she handed him $5.23, then turned away. He realized it would be pointless to protest.

His expression was bleak as he walked out the door. He knew he would never forget the bright yellow light in the barn, and the happiness on the faces of those who had stayed. Over and over the thought kept running through his mind: If I had waited only five seconds more.

Door of Opportunity

Many people in ECK are just like the bank teller. A person will try the spiritual exercises for a while, listen to others talking about how well they work for them, and say, "But they're not working for me." Finally his patience runs out, and he heads for the door. But as he looks back, he sees a beautiful light shining in the faces of those who stayed; and with belated awareness he recognizes their change in consciousness. When he tries to run back in the door, he finds it closed to him.

He must then decide whether or not he has the courage to approach the Master again and ask for another chance to walk this path to God. And often the Master will say, "If you wish to begin to study the ECK discourses again, you may."

So the person begins the whole process all over again. But at some point the doubt returns—What am I doing here? Is it going to work? Yet this time, whenever he is about to leave, he remembers to hang on for only five seconds more.

If we feel ECK is for us, we follow It. Yet we must always have the freedom to say, "This path may not be where I want to spend five seconds more," and walk away without feeling guilty. If you have tried ECK and then feel another path is for you, go to the other path; don't feel guilty. Go where you are happy; go where you belong. The time may come when the other path no longer works for you. And if you want to follow the path of ECK again, the door most likely will be open.

May the blessings be.

Australian Regional Seminar, Melbourne, Australia, Saturday, November 15, 1986

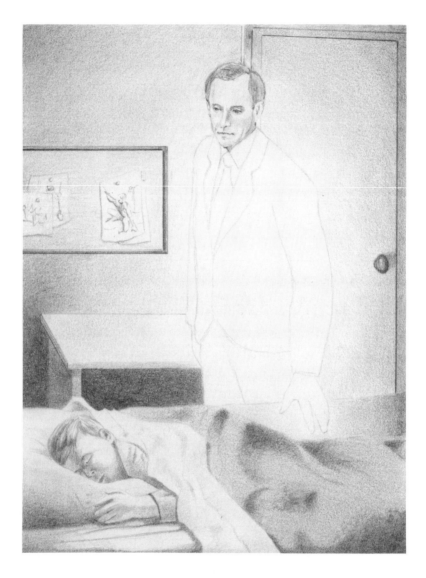

Harold came into my bedroom and said, "You do not need to be scared, for I am with you."

7

Little, but Deep, Healing

The year of spiritual healing has ended, but the effects of it will go on for months. The healings occurred in a number of different ways throughout the year. Sometimes they were physical, but there were also other, more important kinds of healings—those which addressed the deeper causes of the physical problem. These healings took place on the emotional, mental, and spiritual levels.

Often a healing serves to make one more confident, more willing to face life, more eager to wake up each morning and see what experiences life will bring.

How to Brush It Off

A columnist in Chicago took a walk down to the corner with his Quaker friend. They were going to buy a newspaper. At the newsstand his friend held out a dollar bill and asked for a paper. The vendor, a sullen, surly individual, rudely snatched the dollar from his hand and threw the man's change on the counter.

"What a sour person," the columnist remarked to his friend as they left the newsstand. "Why do you keep buying papers from him?"

The other man just shrugged his shoulders. "Why should I react to him?" he asked. What he was really saying was, If someone is having a bad day, that's no reason for mine to be bad, too. The columnist realized then that his friend's way was to act toward people, rather than react, as most of us tend to do. The man displayed good spiritual health.

In ECK we try to find a way to look at the high side of life. It takes a balanced individual to recognize that the world he perceives depends upon his own attitude.

The Grateful Dove

The year of spiritual healing brought healings to animals and birds, too. An ECKist was walking down the street when she heard the shrill sound of screeching brakes. Turning to see what had happened, she noticed a little white dove lying in the road. It had been struck by a car. She started to rush toward it; but two young women in the car quickly jumped out to see if they could help the bird. They knelt and soothed its feathers, trying to give it comfort.

When the ECKist realized it was stunned, not dead, she moved away from the others and whispered softly, "I put you into the hands of Prajapati, the ECK Master who cares for animals. Whatever is to be, will be. The love of ECK be with you." Then she stood back and watched as the two young women gently lifted the dove, put it in their car, and drove off to find a veterinarian for the bird.

About a year later, as the ECKist was walking down the same street, two doves flew down and landed on the sidewalk just ahead of her. One of them limped toward her. Stopping in front of her, it began to make soft cooing sounds. Suddenly she realized this was the same little dove that had been hit by the car a year earlier. The cooing was its way of saying, "I've just come to thank you for the love you gave me when I was injured. The love of ECK goes with you, too."

That done, the bird spread its wings and flew to the roof of a car. It sat there and watched her for a moment before it flew away.

Man in his ignorance likes to pride himself on being God's special creation. He is certain that Soul would make Its home only in a human body. But in ECK we learn that Soul actually takes up residence in all of the body forms around us—in cats, dogs, birds, and all other life.

Broadening Our Concepts

In the time of Galileo, the Italian astronomer was persecuted for daring to suggest that the universe did not revolve around earth. His discovery contradicted the beliefs and teachings of the Church: that earth was the center of all creation. And why not? If God had created man in His own image and placed him on earth, then man and earth had to be the center of all creation. It was all very logical to people in those times.

Studies eventually revealed the true position of the earth in relation to the rest of the solar system. Someday, science may also become convinced not only of the existence of Soul, but that It also resides in forms other than the human body.

Soul is eternal; It has the ability to gain experience in any number of different forms, both on the physical plane and on the inner planes. This concept remains shocking to those who find it more comforting to think of themselves as God's special creation. During the year of spiritual healing, I have tried to broaden the concept of Soul, to move people out of the introversion to which the human consciousness is so accustomed.

As we begin to look outward with this broader view, we can see the Light of God in all creation. Only when the selfishness is gone can understanding and compassion move out to encompass those around us. This is very important.

The African Official

An initiate in Africa described a spiritual healing that happened to another person. In a dream the ECKist saw the leader of his country walking on a beach. Behind him walked the Mahanta, watching over him as a father might watch over a child. The initiate was merely the observer, quietly viewing the dream as it unfolded.

As the two strolled along the sandy beach on the inner planes, the head of state reached into his pocket and pulled out a pack of cigarettes. He removed one from the pack and lit it. With the first puff of smoke, the Mahanta disappeared.

The government official continued his walk, but he knew that something had changed. The farther down the beach he went, the lonelier he felt. He didn't know exactly what had happened, but he could tell that something was missing now.

He didn't realize that the protection that surrounded him had gone away because of his smoking habit. The ECK Masters very seldom put any attention on a person who smokes unless he is making the effort to break the habit. Smoking is one of the habits that block one's spiritual unfoldment and keep him in the lower worlds.

Sometime after the dream had taken place, the ECKist read in the newspaper that this head of state had pronounced a ban on the sale of cigarettes. It seems that he, himself, had quit smoking, and with all the zealousness you might expect from one who has dropped a vice, he now wanted the rest of his countrymen to break the habit, too. Although it hadn't been public knowledge that the head of state was a smoker, the ECKist had seen it in a dream.

The point I'm making here is that the Mahanta, or the higher consciousness of ECK, also works with people beyond the immediate membership of ECKANKAR.

Rising to the Top

Some ECK initiates work in government positions now, and there will be more in the future. ECKists are needed everywhere, in all professions, in all fields throughout the world, including the political arena.

The ECKist is concerned with reaching the heights of spiritual excellence. Whether engaged in an outer office or in spiritual matters—and you can't really separate the two—the ECKist will always rise to the top; he can't help it. This doesn't necessarily mean that he is going to be regarded as a leader by other people, but he will be a leader in spiritual attitudes. If the ECKist isn't actually at the helm, in one way or another he will be there to guide, advise, or assist those who are in a position to make things better for mankind. This is part of the spiritual duties which many ECKists will assume.

The HUing Hygienist

Karma is the reason an individual has problems, and the healings which occur are simply the working off of karma.

A new ECKist worked as a dental hygienist. She learned about the effect of the sound of HU after only two or three months in ECK. Each day at the dentist's office she would silently chant HU and try to keep her attention on the Inner Master. As the weeks passed, her karma began to speed up.

She didn't realize what was happening, but she did notice a strange reaction from the people around her. Co-workers who had once been friends began to gossip about her. Her boss, the dentist, stopped talking to her. It got to the point where going to work was like entering a war zone. Though she couldn't understand why things had changed, through it all she tried to maintain her composure as well as she could.

She couldn't help noticing the difference in herself. In the past, when someone at work got angry with her, she went out of her way to be extra friendly to them. She did everything possible to make amends, just to keep peace. But when it happened now, she just continued to chant HU, the song of God, quietly within herself. At the end of the day she walked out the door and left all the problems behind.

As she left the office one day, she thought about the calm way she had dealt with a particular situation. You are doing quite well as an ECKist, she mused. You didn't react once to all the anger that was thrown at you in there. Comparing it to the way she used to handle such situations, she mentally patted herself on the back. She felt she had made quite a step in her spiritual unfoldment.

Later that evening she went to the grocery store to pick up something for dinner. She felt very lighthearted as she walked through the wintry night and remembered the events of the day. Walking along, she imagined herself having a conversation with the Mahanta. "Thank you so much," she said. "Everything is so different from before." She visualized the Master giving her a bouquet for being such a good girl.

Suddenly a large bouquet of flowers flew past her eyes. It struck the building next to her, bounced off, and landed on the sidewalk in front of her feet. Looking around, she saw that a florist's truck was parked at the curb, and she realized the driver must have thrown out the bouquet.

"Why are you throwing these flowers away?" she called to him.

"They froze in the truck," he explained. "By the time I get them to the store to sell them, they won't be any good."

"Can I have them?" she asked.

"Be my guest," he said.

Gratefully, she picked up the beautiful bouquet of flowers and carried it home. To her it was a gift from the Master, her reward for not letting the anger of other people pull her down to their level.

Effects of the Spiritual Exercises

One of the roles of karma and of the negative power is to pull you down from where you are happy. Its role is to make you feel unhappy, to spoil your day. It makes you want to pull the covers over your head and just stay in bed.

You will get through it more easily if you can realize that the spiritual exercises are helping you to work off your karma. And as each round of karma is worked off, the people around you lose their hold on you; the ropes of karma that have bound you together slacken and must let go.

Something else will happen then: You will find yourself pulled out of this circle of karma and placed in a whole new situation. Usually—though not always—in some way the new place will be a higher station in life, much better than the one you left.

But as you begin working there, a different form of karma will start to work out. This time it may be less of the low-grade karma, because the heat and fire of anger from the Astral Plane is slowly being taken out of your life. You might find that the karma you are facing today is easier to handle. It may involve mental karma, where you run into differences of opinion. But you are calmer now, and the people you work with now are the type who can deal with a problem up front without turning it into a personality conflict.

The further you go in ECK, the more you will notice a change in your outlook and in the people who are drawn to you. This is a very good step. It is part of the spiritual healing which occurs as you practice the spiritual exercises: the Light and Sound of God come into you, and the karma burns off. It really is a very simple process.

Vehicle for Healing

A chiropractor in Minnesota mentioned that he was taking his staff to Florida for a seminar that featured courses on how to perfect their techniques for helping people. Basically, he said, the function of chiropractic is to remove blockages so that the natural life force can get through and do the healing.

I too am concerned with helping the individual get rid of the blockages, which we call karma. As the spiritual blockages are taken away, the natural healing from the ECK takes place.

At the World Wide of ECK seminar in St. Louis, a Higher Initiate was listening to a talk. It occurred to him that he hadn't personally been aware of any kind of spiritual healing going on throughout the year.

Then he noticed that the woman seated next to him

appeared very uncomfortable. She seemed to be trying to move farther away from him, but there wasn't really anywhere to go. Finally she leaned toward him and said, "There is an incredible heat coming from your body." He just looked at her curiously, wondering what she was talking about.

It came to him then that the ECK was using him to heal this woman—whatever her problem was. The heat she felt was the Holy Spirit coming into her through him.

He was pretty pleased with himself. Wow, I healed her! he thought.

Instantly a message came through from the Inner Master. No, you didn't, the inner voice said. You were merely the channel for the healing. At this point, I happened to mention from the stage that a person who is being given a healing by the ECK sometimes feels a tremendous heat.

The point was made to the initiate both on the outer and the inner, and he got the message. So this is what the Year of Spiritual Healing is about, he thought. He felt happy he was able to serve as a channel.

On Sunday morning he attended the Higher Initiates' breakfast. He was just sitting there, enjoying the fellowship, when one of the other Higher Initiates got up to speak. A surge of anger rose within him as soon as he saw who the speaker was. He remembered their first meeting over thirteen years ago, in their early days in ECK. This individual had slighted him in some way, and he had never gotten over it. Even now, the longer he listened to the speaker, the angrier he got.

As he examined his feelings, suddenly it came to him that this hate and anger did not begin just thirteen years ago; it had started a long time ago, back in ancient times. The incident in this lifetime was merely a replay of an event carried over from a past life they had spent together. As quickly as he realized the cause of his anger, it began to melt away.

This Higher Initiate had the insight to recognize that a spiritual healing was occurring, but in a much subtler way than he would have expected. After the talk was over, he found it very easy to go up to the speaker, whom he had avoided all these years, and talk with him as he would to a friend.

Often we feel that a spiritual healing has to cure a physical illness or affliction in order to be valid. This is not true.

Father-Daughter Reunion

Just before the World Wide of ECK seminar in October, an initiate called up his ex-wife. He hadn't spoken to her in many years. Their daughter had been four years old when the couple was divorced, and he hadn't seen the child since. She was now eighteen.

When his ex-wife answered the phone, he got right to the point. "I would like to get together with our daughter," he said. "Do you think she would be willing to see me?"

His ex-wife responded by slamming the phone down, ending the conversation. He gave up on the idea of ever having a chance to meet with his daughter.

Soon after that he went to the seminar. When he returned home a few days later, he found a letter in his mailbox forwarded to him by his sister. It was a letter from his daughter, who had written to her aunt to ask for her father's address. "I would like to contact him," she wrote. Now that she was of age, she had made up her mind to meet him.

Even during the seminar, the initiate had had a feeling

that changes were about to come into his life. Not knowing what they would be, he was a little bit afraid of them. He only hoped he would have the strength to face them. When he found out that his daughter wanted to meet him, he realized it was a gift of love from the Master. In this year of spiritual healing, many of the loose ends left from the past were being allowed to work out.

Healings by the ECK encompass such a broad range that, unless your consciousness is also broad, you may never even realize what the ECK is doing for you.

The Road to SUGMAD

An ECKist moved to a secluded home in a remote mountainous region, preferring the peace and quiet of being far away from his nearest neighbors. One autumn afternoon he got into his four-wheel-drive Jeep and headed out to the main highway to explore the area. He drove along for quite a while, just enjoying the scenery. Finally he decided to see if one of the back roads would provide a shortcut home.

Pulling to the side of the road, he took out his map and studied it. About a mile or two down the highway was a turnoff; the blue line on the map indicated it was a pretty good paved road. Maybe I'll drive down there and see what it's like, he thought. Minutes later he arrived at the turnoff.

The road was in good condition for the first few miles, then suddenly it turned very rough, with branches and logs strewn all along the way. As he maneuvered around them, he began to worry about damaging his vehicle. Should I keep going forward or should I just turn around and go back? he wondered.

The farther he drove, the worse it got, until it became practically impossible to turn around.

Eventually he came to a crossroad which appeared to be in much better condition than the route he was traveling. It seemed to go roughly in the direction of his home. Just as he was tempted to turn onto this road, the voice of the Inner Master, the Mahanta, came through. "Go ahead and go forward."

A little farther down the road he spotted a hawk perched on a low branch. He stopped to get a better look, and saw that the hawk had fresh prey gripped in its beak. He and the bird stared at each other for the longest time. Finally the hawk took flight, circling its way up through the trees to an opening, and disappeared from view. That sure was strange, the ECKist thought.

He started driving again. As he steered the vehicle around a sharp turn, he saw that the road ahead sloped down to a deep marsh. More discouraged than ever, he stopped to consider his options. If he continued on, he would have no choice but to go through the marsh. If he didn't, he would be stranded deep in the woods.

"Go ahead," the inner voice whispered.

Taking a deep breath, he shifted into four-wheel drive and plunged ahead. Fallen branches cracked beneath the wheels and tore at the underside of his vehicle, but he managed to get through the marsh.

At last the long, slow, bumpy journey ended, and he was relieved to find himself turning onto a smooth highway close to home. What a fool you were for taking a road that bad, he thought to himself. You could have gotten lost in there. It would have been days before anyone found you. Don't you have any sense at all?

But thinking it over later, he realized that an outer experience so graphic, filled with such distinct visual impressions, must have some spiritual significance. Could the Inner Master be using his adventure as a way to give him an insight into his progress on the spiritual path?

He began to reflect on the various aspects of his journey, each incident taking on new meaning as he related it to the ECK. The rough road symbolized the way back to SUGMAD. The crossroads were actually the way of Kal, which gives the illusion of being smoother and better than the bumpy ECK way. The hawk represented the Mahanta, and the captured prey a blockage that had been in the way. When the bird flew off, taking the prey with him, it meant that the Mahanta was removing the blockage. The inner voice was Soul urging him to continue the journey home to SUGMAD.

He felt the obstacle-filled marsh exemplified the different tests which occur to try to dishearten a person and make him want to turn back. But after a certain point on the path, you are on your way home to God; there is no turning back. Knowing this, he was able to ignore his doubts. He listened to his inner voice and continued straight ahead.

He now saw that the experience as a whole represented Soul marching boldly through the illusory worlds of mind, seeking the SUGMAD.

A Shorter Shariyat Technique

At the World Wide of ECK, I presented a spiritual exercise which I call the Shariyat technique. Seldom do I repeat a technique I've already given, but this one has proven to be very helpful to those who have been in ECK for a while but have had little or no success with experiencing the Light and Sound.

Some of you have difficulty with the imaginative techniques because of your practical, down-to-earth nature.

Whenever you try to use your imagination, you stop to wonder: Is this real or not? As soon as the mind starts to dissect the experience, the benefit of the spiritual exercise is lost, and you can't turn the corner.

So, if you have a problem but you don't know quite how to go about solving it because you can't make contact with the Inner Master on the inner planes, you might want to try the Shariyat technique. This version, which has four parts, is shorter and even easier to work with than the one given at the World Wide.

The first step is simply to look at whatever problem you are having, whether it involves a spiritual matter, physical health, finances, a broken heart, or anything of this nature.

Second, open Book One or Two of *The Shariyat-Ki-SUGMAD* at random and read a paragraph.

The third step is to chant HU and contemplate upon what you have just read in *The Shariyat*. Don't contemplate on your problem or try to make some kind of a bridge between the paragraph and your problem. This is very important. Just contemplate upon the paragraph from *The Shariyat* while chanting HU.

After you have completed the contemplation, the fourth step is to open *The Shariyat*, again at random, and read another paragraph. At this point, you can try to see how the first and second paragraphs relate to your problem. The entire exercise shouldn't go much longer than fifteen or twenty minutes.

The following day, if you still don't have an answer, do the spiritual exercise again. If you do get an answer, then you can use the same technique on another problem that may be bothering you. Some of you will get your answer very quickly, maybe even the first time, but others may have to work at it for up to a month before it comes.

Getting Your Secret Word

An ECK initiate had been concerned about his lack of progress in ECK. He decided to take this spiritual problem into the inner planes via the Shariyat technique. On the third day of using this spiritual exercise, he got his answer.

It came to him very clearly that the reason for his lack of spiritual success was that he had not gotten a secret word at his last initiation. It hadn't seemed that important at the time, but with his new insight he proceeded to find his word.

In such cases, or if you got a secret word but it no longer works, it is not necessary to go back to the Initiator. This is because ECK is an inner-directed path. Go to the Inner Master instead, and ask for another secret word.

One way to get the word is through the Shariyat technique. Simply state your problem: I seem to have outgrown my secret word for now. It no longer seems to work. I may come back to it later, but for now I would like to have a new one.

Once you have stated the problem as you see it, forget about it and go on to the next step. Open *The Shariyat* at random, read a paragraph, and contemplate upon what you have read. Then open *The Shariyat* again and read another paragraph. Through the Golden-tongued Wisdom, which is an aspect of the ECK-Vidya, the ancient science of prophecy, the two paragraphs should present some kind of an answer.

Contacting the Inner Master

I would like to remind you that no matter where you go or what you do, I am always with you. Not in this physical body, but as the Inner Master. The Inner Master

127

is the central core of the ECK teachings, and this body is merely the outer representation of the inner being.

An ECK initiate handed me this story by one of our youngest ECK writers. The title is "The Storm Got Bigger."

It was one dark night. All was calm. Not a sound was to be said [sic]. The wind was blowing so much that the sea was rough. In the morning all of the sand was black. I was in my bed all alone. I said to myself, "Harold, please, I do not like to be on my own in the nighttime." Harold came into my bedroom and said, "You do not need to be scared, for I am with you." Then he left. The end.

Always remember, as this young writer knows, that once you make contact with the Inner Master, you need never be alone. The love of the ECK, the Holy Spirit, and God is with you everywhere, under any conditions, at all times.

Australian Regional Seminar, Melbourne, Australia,
Sunday, November 16, 1986

I watched the other skaters, because you can learn a lot from people who know how to do things better.

8

How the ECK Works Every Day

Recently some people began to make a connection between the weather and ECKANKAR's move to Minneapolis. Tentative jokes started in December, but it was a little too early to definitely conclude that we might have been the cause of one of the mildest Minnesota winters in over a century. Some natives even called it "the winter that wasn't."

Winter Stories

In March we finally got about a foot of snow. "This is quite a snowstorm," we complained to the Minnesota natives.

They just brushed it off. "It didn't last but a day and a half," they said. "It doesn't count."

When they'd tell us stories about their severe winters, we'd say "Oh, we're sure your winters are very bad," then cast meaningful glances at the snowless ground. That really aggravated them. "Just you wait!" they assured us. Well, we did.

Some not-so-happy news from Minnesota concerns the radio program, "A Prairie Home Companion." It will be closing its doors in June. I've always admired that program. Garrison Keillor's portrayal of the residents of Lake Wobegon actually had deep spiritual insight into the way people live and face their problems every day. He has a rare gift for imparting the humbleness of life to a culture that moves so fast, many people find it difficult to keep up.

While I was at a car wash near the end of the winter, I asked the cashier, "Do you always have mild winters like this?" I was kind of goading her.

"Actually, no," she said. "This is a very rare occurrence." But, she explained, she knew why the winter was so mild.

"Why is that?"

"Because my car heater was broken," she said. That sounded as good as anything else I'd heard so far.

Garrison Keillor had pointed out that when the weather turns unseasonably warm in the north, people don't know quite what to make of it. They lose their sense of direction. It doesn't feel right. They can't think clearly when the winter is that warm.

A meteorologist was recently interviewed on a radio talk show. In researching the weather records dating back 168 years, he found that the last time Minnesota had such a warm winter was in the early 1800s. So, based on records over a 168-year span, the earlier ones of which were very poorly kept, he deduced that the next time Minnesota would enjoy so mild a winter would be about the year 2050. It was an amazing conclusion considering the lack of facts; most of us won't be around as witnesses to see if he is right.

Ice-Skating Lesson

This past winter I went ice skating for the first time in many years. Though there wasn't much snow, at times it got cold enough to freeze the water in the little rink by the local softball field, which provided very good skating. My new ice skates were so stiff at first that it was like wearing cold steel on my feet. Rubbing some oil into the heels helped.

The skating went pretty well, though I did get out of breath—something I don't recall happening when I was younger. But after a little bit of practice I got into some fancy steps, crossing one leg over the other and going around in a nice circle. I was moving right along.

At the same time I watched the other skaters, because you can learn a lot from people who know how to do things better. Right next to the skating rink used by the general public was an ice-hockey rink. Hockey players are the real skating experts, moving effortlessly backward, forward, sideways, and in any other direction they please. I watched in admiration as one guy glided backward, very casually reaching his hockey stick toward the puck as it came toward him. So I practiced skating backward too.

Then he went forward, jumped slightly, did a little turn in the air, and landed while skating backward. I just had to give that one a try.

With the windchill factor at minus thirty degrees that day, only my two eyes peeked out over the scarf wrapped up to my nose. But I started out skating into the wind, because it slowed me down. First I went forward, did a little turn, then skated backward. It went so well that I did it again. Soon I felt confident enough to turn around and skate with the wind, which meant I was going much faster. I had it down to an art form—go forward fast, do a little hop in the air, twist to the left, then skate backward.

Now I was ready to try it with a turn to the right. Going forward really fast, I jumped up in the air a little bit, turned to the right—and landed on the ice in a twisted pile of arms and legs and feet. Did you ever notice that the ice is much harder when you jump up in the air and aggravate it?

As I limped home, I thought about what I had done wrong. First of all, I learned how to do something new by watching someone else. That part was OK. It went fine when I did the turn in one direction. So far, so good. But when I tried to turn the other way, it didn't work. Why? Because even though it looked the same both ways, it was a totally different move.

If you are going to try something new, it's best to slow down first and learn it the right way. Most of the lessons the ECK teaches us are like this. We often start out feeling we can't do something: We think we're too old, it's beneath our dignity, or other people will laugh at us. Then one day Soul says, "I'm tired of being afraid. I'm tired of worrying about what other people will think."

So we start by observing the experts, much as one would watch how a Master does something in life. But once we have learned to do it a certain way and want to go on to something new, we often forget to slow down before making a change. This is when we find that the ground is very hard when we fall.

I later learned that when the other skaters started to teeter, they didn't wait until the last minute when they had no choice but to fall. Instead, they gracefully eased themselves down on the ice. I wish I had been smart enough to think of that.

Is This God?

An initiate told me about an experience she'd had as a six-year-old child. She woke up in the dream state and saw two big eyes staring out of a gigantic head that covered the entire sky. The skin of this enormous head was pulsing with light. It had to be God, she figured; and if so, she wanted no part of it. The vision was so frightening that she backed away from religion for years until she came into ECK.

A lot of people claim to have knowledge of the beings and deities on the other planes. They often believe they are having direct contact with God. But one can never actually see God. What can be known are the two aspects of the Holy Spirit—the ECK—which are Light and Sound. Nor can we ever become God, but we can become Godlike through having the God-Consciousness.

The vision seen by the six-year-old child was just Jehovah. In ECK we call him Jot Niranjan; he's a deity on the lower rungs of the spiritual hierarchy. Each of these beings has a place. They all serve the highest deity and do the best they can, because they too are unfolding into the higher realms of spirituality. This is often forgotten by the followers of Christianity, who feel that the expansion of consciousness won't affect their concept of God. But it will.

A Balanced Life

One of the Higher Initiates recently moved to a small town where everybody was a Baptist. "You're a nobody in this town unless you're a Baptist," she told us. "Furthermore, everybody makes it a point to ask which church you go to. Knowing how they feel, I'm not sure how to answer them."

"Why not just say, 'the nearest one,'" my wife suggested. She's very practical.

A retired couple who had just moved to a small town

ran into a similar situation. "If you don't belong to a church," they wrote, "you are totally ostracized. No one will have anything to do with you." They wondered if it would hurt their spiritual unfoldment to join the neighborhood church.

We are looking for a balanced life where we can be vehicles for the ECK, and it's difficult to do that in a town where you aren't accepted by the people. So I said, "If this is where you can be an ECK channel and this is what you feel you would like to do, then by all means, go ahead." In some cases, you may have to do just that.

Cultural Changes

I was talking with the ECK Youth Council about how the ECK works in everyday life and how It fills the needs of each individual who comes to this path. I also pointed out that there has been a major social revolution going on over the last seven or eight decades. World War I gave rise not only to a leisure class—the middle class—but also to child-labor laws. The period surrounding World War I, in fact, is when the concept of teenagers as a specialized category of people began to unfold.

Before the war the United States was an agricultural society. But with the onset of the war, the American soldiers went off to Europe, saw more of the world, and got a taste of the big cities like London and Paris. Thus, they returned home and entered the postwar period with visions of a different life. No longer content to go back to the farm, they moved to the cities, raised families there, and tried to assimilate into a different cultural environment.

But now the children didn't have the duties of the old days to occupy them. On the farm, children were needed for the day-to-day survival of the family—to help raise and harvest the crops, take care of the cattle, bring in the wood, and so on. This was no longer the case. Furthermore, the child-labor laws prevented them from having to work under inhumane conditions in places like textile factories. Before these laws were passed they had to work long hours, starting before the sun came up and staying until after dark, in shops where the only illumination came from candlelight. Many lost their eyesight at an early age. In fact, life in general was very difficult for the people who incarnated during those times.

When the child-labor laws restricted the employment of children in the cities, it became very difficult to figure out what to do with them. Regular school attendance began to take on more importance, but that still left plenty of leisure time after school let out. This huge change in the cultural patterns, which took place within a decade or two, led to the expansion of youth organizations such as the YMCA and the Boy Scouts.

Today the situation is undergoing another significant change. With television and video games, it's a whole different culture. The question now is: How will we in ECK meet the needs of the ECK youth of today and those to come in the future? This is going to be quite an undertaking for youth and adults alike.

Video Games

Usually I get up early in the morning and spend the whole day writing and doing whatever else needs to be done. But sometimes when the ECK comes through too strongly, I promise myself a treat: As soon as the work is finished, I can go out and play a game of Ms. Pac-Man!

Watching the kids play the video games, it might appear that such games are purely destructive, but they are actually part of the educational processes which help today's youth learn the lessons of life. I used to say, "What an artificial way to look at life," until I realized just how many lessons were being taught. They actually learn some very good principles and get to practice putting them into action.

The games teach them, for instance, about the obstacles that life can throw at you, and how to overcome them. They also learn that if you want something, you have to pay for it. That means coming up with a quarter. And until you become good at the game, it's going to cost you a lot of quarters. Since most kids aren't rich, they have to get good.

As a beginner just learning to play a game, you use up a lot of quarters. But if you become proficient at one level, you can advance to the next level. Even if you don't have too many quarters to spend, you can still watch others play.

Often you'll hear the more experienced players sharing the little tricks of the game. "Watch out for this. Watch out for that," they tell their friends. This is what the Mahanta, the Living ECK Master does, too. Through the inner communication and the outer writings, he shows you what to watch out for—if you'll only listen. Otherwise, some things can gobble you up.

I can warn you about the five passions of the mind, but just talking about them is not good enough; they're just terms. You have to go through it. You have to play the game yourself.

Gaining Compassion

A Higher Initiate went through an unusual phase of being very frightened at night. Her nerves were so on edge that she wouldn't go to bed without leaving the television on for company. About the same time she started reading mystery novels; they seemed to help keep her attention off of her fears. Such fearful behavior was so completely against her nature that she couldn't figure out what had come over her.

One evening she went to visit her mother, an elderly woman who suffered from Parkinson's disease. She was quite surprised to find the bedroom floor littered with mystery stories and the TV going full blast.

"What's going on?" she asked.

Her mother explained that some of the medication she was taking produced symptoms of unreasonable, unaccountable fear. Her doctor had suggested that she try watching television and reading books to occupy her mind.

The ECK had arranged for the Higher Initiate to experience what it felt like to be on this medication. Now that she understood what her mother was going through, she could relate to the older woman with real compassion.

Life has a way of putting you in a position to know and understand exactly what it feels like to walk in someone else's shoes. This is one reason why it's best not to criticize and gossip about another, because as sure as you do, you're going to find yourself walking in his shoes. You can bet on it. It's just a matter of time.

Over and over I've observed what happens to people who display a self-righteous attitude about certain problems another person has stumbled into. Pretty soon they find themselves going through the very same problem that they were so sure the other person could have avoided. The funny thing is, they rarely see the connection between their attitude and what has befallen them. These experiences are all part of your spiritual training, but you are not always aware of what is happening while you're going through it.

An Admirer of Eisenhower

Sometimes the ECK tries to teach us how to be greater by steering our attention toward someone who is great in his field. Someone who, whether he knows it or not, is guided by the spiritual principles. It might be a better video-game player, or a great political leader, business leader, spiritual leader—whatever.

One morning I was nervously awaiting my turn in the dentist's chair when the door to the inner office opened and an elderly gentleman came out. He was rather a gabby person, eager to strike up a conversation with anybody who looked his way. Instead of leaving right away, he sat down next to me and began to talk about his days on the staff of General Dwight D. Eisenhower, who was the leader of the Allied forces in Europe during World War II.

Always an admirer of President Eisenhower, I was very interested in what the man had to say.

What impressed him the most about Eisenhower, he said, was the man's ability to make each individual feel he was talking directly to him, even if he was speaking before a crowd of two thousand. He also mentioned that as a general, and later as president, even if he originated an idea himself, Eisenhower always gave the credit to someone else. He truly was a humble man.

His spirit of cooperation is what made him, I feel, one of the country's greater presidents. Those who remember his relatively passive presidency, which came in the quiet after the two world wars and the Korean War, might wonder what he did that was so great. During his terms in office, America saw the highest levels of prosperity in many decades. This is not to say that Eisenhower was necessarily responsible for it, but he did have the spiritual quality of allowing his staff to work with freedom.

Though he freely delegated authority to subordinates, when he saw the need for something to be done a certain way, he would take action. This is similar to what we learn in ECK. There is a time to step forward and take charge, and, when we have exhausted our own efforts, there is a time to step back and let the ECK take over.

Chasing the Goose

When he was about five years old, Eisenhower was sent for a visit to his aunt's farm, where he found himself in the midst of all these strangers who were his relatives. He couldn't wait to go outside and explore the farm. Armed with a warning to steer clear of the well, little Ike walked around in front of the house for a while, then went around to the back.

Over near the barn he spotted the most wonderful bird he had ever seen—a huge goose. He hurried over to get a closer look. As soon as he got near enough, the goose suddenly came charging at him, wings flapping, hissing, squawking, and making all kinds of scary noises.

Ike ran all the way back to the house, yelling that a goose was attacking him. His relatives assured him that there was nothing to worry about and sent him back outside to play. Once again, the goose chased him back inside. This happened several times.

Finally his uncle decided to intervene. But he didn't go out there and hit the goose over the head or chase it away. Instead, much as an ECK Master would do it, he gave Ike some tips on how to deal with the situation. "Come over here," he said to the boy. "I have something to show you."

From a closet he produced an old broom with the bristles worn down. With a pair of shears, he cut off the rest of the bristles, leaving just a little stub on the end. "Now you've got a stick," he said. "Come outside, and I'll show you how to use it."

Out in the yard his uncle instructed Ike in the art of swinging the broomstick. "Now show me what you're going to do the next time the goose comes after you," he said, handing it to Ike. The five-year-old grasped the handle and began to swing the broom around clumsily. Soon he got pretty good at it. "You can go anywhere you want to now," his uncle said. "Next time that goose comes after you, just chase him with the stick." Little Ike shuddered at the thought. Much later it occurred to him that his uncle had greatly overestimated his courage.

His uncle went in the house and left Ike outside with the broomstick. As soon as he saw the goose coming, he panicked. Without waiting to see what the bird was going to do, the boy let out a yell and went tearing after him, waving the broomstick in the air, shouting at the top of his lungs. When the goose saw this noisy little tornado coming at him, he quickly turned around and ran the other way, squawking—but not before Ike got in a few good licks on his tail feathers.

Now that the boy knew how to deal with this obstacle, after that he was able to go outside and play in safety— as long as he carried his broomstick.

The ECK's Way

Occasionally I get letters from initiates who say that someone is causing this or that problem in their area. They wonder why I don't step in and do something. Usually I don't like to interfere. In one case a person was doing

142

certain things which were not in accord with the ECK teachings. I tried to work it out by having Spiritual Services at the ECK Office write a letter to the individual. But other than to aggravate him, it had very little effect. He just kept on doing the same things because, like so many others, he thought I didn't know.

I waited almost a year and a half before taking action, simply because I wanted to give him enough time and room to turn around on his own. Finally it got to the point where I had to sit down and write him a letter myself. Very reasonably I stated what I had heard. "This is not befitting a person of your spiritual station," I wrote. "Is it true, or have the reports been wrong?"

The individual wrote back and admitted that the reports were true. But, he explained, he just had not realized the impact of what he was doing. He was very surprised to hear directly from me. Like many people, he was not aware that such things always come to my attention.

Sometimes we can get so caught up in the rightness of our own actions that it takes a broomstick to knock any sense into us. But it's just the ECK's way of coming in through the back door, through the hard knocks of life, to show us what we missed and what must be learned if we are to progress.

Dream Study

There are many books on dream interpretation that carry impressive-sounding titles. They promise ten thousand dreams explained or ten thousand symbols revealed. In actual fact, when's the last time you had a dream about an ostrich or a claw hammer? Since the chances of seeing such images are practically nonexistent, I think it's safe to say that most of these books are not very useful.

The ECK dream discourses are based on many of the things I learned firsthand through experiences in the dream state. They may not fit what everybody else has learned, but I believe many people will find them helpful.

The discourses and many of our new ECK books give examples in story form of how the ECK works in everyday life. The lessons of life can best be expressed, and are more likely to be remembered, when told in story format. It is a very effective way to present the ECK teachings, whether in print or through the spoken word.

May the blessings be.

ECKANKAR International Youth Conference, New York, New York, Friday, April 17, 1987

Why is the sailor hesitating? Because suddenly he finds himself faced with a major dilemma. Here on this small island he is the undisputed king.

9

The Hundredth Monkey

I sincerely wish I could say the words about the Sound and Light that would give each of you instant upliftment to the Soul Plane. Unfortunately, it isn't that easy. Unfoldment is a twofold process: First you have to know the way, and then you have to walk it.

The Living ECK Master can show the way through examples and spiritual exercises to help open the consciousness. But if the individual truly wants the enlightenment which leads him closer home to God, it is up to him to accept the trust which has been given to him and walk the path himself.

The Little King

I saw an interesting cartoon in a magazine. A sailor is shipwrecked on a desert island. There used to be two trees on the island, but the sailor has cut one down to make himself a chair. Oddly enough, the chair is constructed in the shape of a throne.

An officer from a huge freighter, shown anchored off in the distance, has rowed to shore to rescue the sailor. But instead of rushing gratefully into the boat that has

147

come to take him back home, the sailor remains seated in his throne. Silently he watches three monkeys who are bowing down before him with their faces in the sand.

"Make up your mind," the officer says. "Do you want to be rescued or not?"

Why is the sailor hesitating? Because suddenly he finds himself faced with a major dilemma. Here on this small island he is the undisputed king. But if he gets on the freighter and goes back to civilization, what will he be there?

Often it's that way with us, too. In many different lives, we, as Soul, are given an opportunity to leave our own little islands. At first we don't want to go. We've become locked in our little lives, enamored with our own little victories, attracted by the antics in our own little worlds where we are the king. Then at some point, along comes the Master in the good ship ECKANKAR. He goes out in a little boat, rows closer and closer, and finally comes ashore. He knows what we're up against—he sees the three monkeys bowing before us—but still he says, "I've got a way for you to get off this island and go back to civilization."

So now we have to make a choice: Do we want to give up our familiar lives and go off to a far greater place of which we have only a dim memory? Are we willing to leave this small world to venture into the God Worlds?

Presented with this opportunity to leave the known for the unknown, most people say, "Set sail—I'm staying." The monkeys are so happy that they jump up and down, bring out the bananas, and have a party. But as the weeks pass, their antics start to grow old—it can get pretty dull watching them pick fleas off one another. Finally you get to the point where you wish for the next ship to come, for you are ready now to take the voyage home to God. This is when the spiritual journey begins in earnest.

The ECK works in a number of different ways. We humans like to think we make our own plans for how something should come about. But in truth, if it isn't in conjunction with the overall plan of the ECK, it will be rearranged so that the ECK's work will be done first. You can catch up with your own life later, and that will work out fine, too.

A Good Editor

A new book we wanted to publish—*How I Learned Soul Travel*—got sidetracked for a while because of the move to Minnesota. One day we looked at it again and decided that the most likely window for its release was the upcoming Creative Arts Festival. But with the office editorial staff so busy on other projects, it seemed impossible to make the deadline.

An ECK initiate in California, whom we knew to be a very good editor, was asked if she would be willing to tackle the project. She said she would be very happy to do it, but her teaching job involved several upcoming classes which might interfere with the deadline. "I'll do the best I can to work it into my schedule," she promised us.

"Fine," we said. "Whenever you can start, just let us know."

Shortly after that we got a call from her. Her voice was so hoarse that we could barely make out what she was saying. The gist of it was that she had come down with a bad case of laryngitis which had forced her to postpone her classes. Now she had plenty of time on her hands. After croaking out an assurance that she felt fine in every other way, she asked us to send her the manuscript so she could begin work right away. Knowing how the ECK works, she estimated that her laryngitis would last as long as it took to edit the book—and she was right. When the project was completed, she proceeded to catch up with her other commitments, and everything worked out.

Those who serve the ECK are able to see the miracles that take place when something needs to be done. About all you can say is, "I am thy humble servant, SUGMAD."

Principle of Love

In the past, ECKists who wanted to bring themselves closer to the Holy Spirit started the morning by saying, "I am a vehicle for the SUGMAD, the ECK, and the Mahanta." They would then meet the day knowing that everything was being accomplished as it should. But in the meantime, the expansion of consciousness began to bring about a change, and pretty soon the words became a postulate which more directly reflects the principle of the love of God. It goes like this: "I love the SUGMAD, the ECK, and the Mahanta." It means that you are in this state of being at all times.

When I brought this up earlier in a meeting with the Higher Initiates, one woman mentioned that she had already begun to say it that way on her own. Before that, she had felt like an empty channel through which the love passed, and she never got any.

You are not like an empty pan on the stove that has to wait to be filled with soup before it's of any use. You are Soul—a unit, or spark, of God. And as such you are a unit of divine love. Therefore, if you place yourself in this state—if you love the SUGMAD (God), the ECK (Holy Spirit), and the Mahanta (the state of consciousness which is a bridge between the human and the God state)—then all things will come to you. If you love, you can meet each day with joy. Don't feel you must wait around before you can be a worthwhile child of God. You already are.

Shaping Destiny

Most of the people who have helped shape the destiny of the human race have been guided by the Holy Spirit, whether they were conscious of this influence or not. Abraham Lincoln is a wonderful example for anyone who aspires to spiritual unfoldment. As you read and learn about him, you can see how the ECK worked in his life.

Lincoln certainly had his share of experiences with the higher state of consciousness, but he didn't understand what they meant. One example is the time he looked in the mirror and saw a duplicate reflection of his face, which he described as being about four inches lower than his physical face. Without realizing what was going on, he had slipped into the astral consciousness where he could actually see his Astral body.

Operating from this level of awareness aroused in Lincoln a great sympathy for the downtrodden, the poor, and the suffering. He became a champion in the crusade for human freedom. Though he also worked for women's suffrage and other areas of human rights, his main purpose for coming into that life was to bring freedom to those held in slavery. The circumstances of the times led him to issue the Emancipation Proclamation, which dealt a deathblow to human bondage.

It took many years before his policies evolved into even a shadow of their original intent, and, despite their lasting influence overall, to this day mankind still slips backward. But it isn't the mission of the ECK Masters to bring an upliftment in the social consciousness; these are missions for the social saviors such as Lincoln. The ECK Masters come to bring liberation from the whole condition of the lower worlds, from the whole human consciousness.

Abe and the Ground Squirrel

When Abe Lincoln was practicing law in Springfield, Illinois, lawyers would follow a judge from town to town, wherever he held court. Lincoln and the other lawyers would often gather at a hotel near the courthouse and pass the time by sharing stories with each other. Lincoln's stories, always told with such humor and intelligence, were enjoyed by everybody.

One afternoon he and his cohorts met at a hotel for some food and drink. As usual, none of them had much money.

"You look like a sorry lot," observed the innkeeper. "Do any of you have enough to pay the bill?"

"Don't worry about it," Lincoln said. "Just take our orders, and by the time you come back we'll have figured out who's going to pay for all this."

"I have an idea," said one of the lawyers, a man whose inclination to talk at length on any subject had earned him the nickname of Know-All. "Each of us will ask a question, and if no one else can answer it, then the one who asked it must give the answer. The first person who can't answer his own question has to pay for the meals."

Everyone agreed to these terms, and Lincoln went first.

Drawing their attention to a ground squirrel's hole right outside the window, he asked the others, "Why is there no dirt around the hole?"

The lawyers discussed it from every angle, but no one could figure it out. Finally Know-All said, "That's your question, Abe. You answer it."

Lincoln said, "There's no dirt around the hole because the ground squirrel began digging at the bottom."

"But how did he get to the bottom to commence digging?" asked Know-All.

"That's your question," Lincoln said. "You answer it."

Abraham Lincoln was actually a very funny man, but as the duties of the presidency began to weigh on him, the humor didn't always show. He also had a very sharp intellect, which is how the ECK comes through as one works on the Mental Plane. He consistently came up with clever ways to work out difficult situations, occasionally even finding himself in the role of Solomon.

House-Paint Compromise

While he was still practicing law, a farmer came to Lincoln's office, obviously very upset. "Sir," the man said, "I want to file for divorce."

"Why?" Lincoln asked.

"My wife and I used to get along very well," the farmer began. "We lived in a log cabin at first, but as times got better, we were able to build ourselves a nice frame house."

Lincoln was puzzled. "A lot of people would be happy to move from a log cabin to a frame house," he said. "So what's the problem?"

The farmer said, "I want to paint the house white like the rest of our neighbors, but my wife wants to paint it brown."

"That sounds easy enough to resolve," Lincoln said. "Why don't you just figure out some compromise?"

"It's way beyond that," the farmer said. "What began as a mild dispute has turned into a violent argument. She's broken dishes over my head and even poured hot water down my back!"

Abe Lincoln thought it over for a moment. Finally he said, "Surely you must have learned something from life. There has to be some solution to this problem. Before you do anything drastic, why not go home and try to work out a compromise?"

The farmer was reluctant. As far as he was concerned, it was a lost cause. "At least give it a try," Lincoln urged. "Then come back in a month, and we'll talk again."

Four weeks later the farmer returned to Lincoln's office. "It all worked out," he announced.

"You and your wife reached a compromise?" Lincoln asked. He was always eager to hear how his advice turned out.

"We sure did," the man said, looking mighty pleased with himself.

"How did you do it?"

The farmer said. "We agreed to paint the house brown."

It Takes Two Sides

We go through life wanting things our own way. But all too often we run into others who disagree with us. Words lead to more words, until finally we are in such a predicament that we can't back off—to do so would mean we'd lose face. Yet, one of the biggest lessons we can learn in ECK is to do everything possible to reach an accord with the individual with whom we are having a problem. But that doesn't mean it's always going to work.

After lengthy negotiations between the United States and Russia fell through, the media approached John Foster Dulles, secretary of state during the Eisenhower administration, and demanded an explanation.

"Why did you let the negotiations fail?" they asked.

"Gentlemen," he said, "it takes two sides to reach an agreement."

In ECK, as we come out of the childhood of spirituality and move into the greater states of awareness, we learn to let other people be. So even when it simply is not possible to reach an agreement, we can still figure out ways to make the situation livable for ourself and others. Saving face is an important element in a person's self-esteem. This factor may not be as sharply defined in our culture as in places like the Orient and the Pacific islands, yet the leaders in ECK must take it into consideration when working with others.

Ike's Lesson

President Eisenhower was another individual who did much for the United States. In his own way, he was a spiritual giant. Working first in the military and later in the political field, he served his country for forty-five years out of a sense of duty rather than self-gain.

When his second term of office had ended, he published a book of reminiscences and used the first royalty check to buy a car. His comment as he showed the car to his wife, Mamie, was: "Here is the fruit of forty-five years' work." He was not one to take more than the office offered or required.

President Eisenhower, or Ike, learned many lessons in his youth, just as we do in the adolescence of our spirituality. As a young man he got an appointment to West Point, the U.S. Military Academy. He put in his time as a *plebe,* a first-year student, enduring the requisite shagging and hazing from upperclassmen. This is the practice of harassing the newest cadets by sending them off on errands from one end of the campus to the other and making them perform all kinds of menial jobs.

The religious school I attended as a youth was a watered-down version of West Point. They adopted some of the academy's principles, then managed to distort and corrupt the worst of them. Shagging and hazing were pretty well corrupted by the time I got there. At West Point, however, these methods were used to weed out those who were not fit or strong enough to be officer material, and indeed many first-year students quit and went home.

Ike then entered the second year, at which point he advanced to the status of *yearling*. He recalled the time one of the plebes came racing down the campus street on an errand for an upperclassman and collided headlong into him. The impact knocked the other guy to the ground. As a yearling, Ike felt duty-bound to mock up anger and make sarcastic remarks.

He stood back and studied the plebe sprawled on the street, and tried to come up with an effective insult. Finally, with all the contempt he could muster, he said, "You look like a—a *barber!*"

The young man got up slowly and addressed Eisenhower in a soft, embarrassed voice. "Sir," he said, "I am a barber."

This quiet statement shocked Eisenhower badly, but he didn't yet have the grace to apologize. Instead, he made some feeble joke about it. Then he turned around, went straight to his room, and told his roommate, "I've just done something stupid and unforgivable. I've managed to make a man ashamed of the work he did to earn a living." He vowed he would never again engage in the shagging and hazing of another person, even if it meant being drummed out of West Point. And he kept his word.

As Soul, we too learn our lessons in the very hardest way. All too often we blunder and make statements that offend other people, simply because we have never been in their position. It behooves us to be careful of the words we speak and the thoughts we think, and not give vanity free rein.

To put ourself in a position to mock or make fun of someone else is vanity and anger walking hand in hand. Then you can absolutely bet on the wheel of karma turning until the situations and settings are perfectly right. The day will come when you find yourself learning just what it feels like to wear the other person's shoes.

Self-Survival

So even if you have no other motive for considering the feelings of others and allowing them their space, do it for self-survival. This is a selfish motive, of course, but it's a start. As we go further along in our journey home to God and are bruised by life more and more, the edges of vanity and I-ness are beat out of us. Finally, only love remains. Once we reach this turning point in our spiritual unfoldment, we begin to treat the people in our life with love instead of fear, anger, or vanity. We have sympathy, compassion, tolerance, and the willingness to go one more step. No longer out of duty or fear, our willingness now springs from love. This is when we can truly say we have made a very important step on the path back home to God.

Sometimes people take themselves so seriously that they get all tied up. You can't hurry the process of unfoldment. But if you are aware that the expanded consciousness exists—that at the end of all things is love, and that at some point love will begin to direct all your actions and thoughts—then you can go ahead and live your life with ease.

You can accept that there will be times when you have to run and times when you have to slow down. Inwardly you are always going at your own pace, marching to the beat of your own drummer. This attitude will never be understood by anyone who remains subject to fear or any of the five passions of the mind which try to take control.

One Billion Chinese

A former player on the University of North Carolina basketball team explained why he had such fond memories of his coach. The coach was a very wise man named Smith. Years ago, before a particularly big game, the team was very much on edge. During the pregame warm-ups they couldn't make any baskets; they even missed passes to each other. Everything went wrong. The team was so nervous that even their opponents and the spectators could see it.

Just before the game began, the coach called the players into a huddle. "Now, boys, I want you to remember something," he said. "There are over one billion Chinese in the world who are never even going to know that you played this game tonight. So go out there now and have a good time." And they did.

I don't know if they won the game that night, but they were winners in one sense: They realized that if they didn't take life so seriously, they could go out there and enjoy it. This is what we are trying to do, too, as we learn to work within the Light and Sound of ECK.

Vibrations of ECK

The ECK is the Holy Spirit, the Voice of God, which can be heard as Sound and seen as Light. Unlike many religions, in ECK we do not experience the Holy Spirit as a great emotional state that comes upon you with such a

158

burst of feeling that you go around singing hosanna. We are referring to something entirely different — spiritually clean, not murky.

The Sound and Light are very real in ECK. The Light we speak of is the manifestation of the Holy Spirit at a certain rate of vibration. It's a rate of vibration in which the atoms of God can be seen. As these atoms move faster at a higher level of vibration, they can be heard as the Sound Current of ECK.

The Light is seen in many different ways, depending upon the individual's state of consciousness. It may come as a blue flash, like flashbulbs going off, or as a blue globe which looks like a very steady small blue light. This is known as the Blue Light of the Mahanta. Another form is the white light or a yellowish-white light. Sometimes it looks like the sun but much more brilliant and pure. It can be seen as a green, lavender, or pink light. Jakob Böhme, the mystic cobbler, saw everything with an aura of pinkness about it, which is one of the preliminary stages of the Light of God. Any of these manifestations simply means that the Light of God is coming to show Soul the way home to the heavenly kingdom, to the Godhead.

The Sound does not come as the voice of an awesome deity speaking to you. Instead, depending upon your level of consciousness during contemplation or in the dream state, It can come in the form of music, the different sounds of nature, or any number of ways. For instance, you might hear It as the buzzing of insects, the twittering of birds, the tinkling of bells, or musical instruments. What it means is that, at this particular time, the Sound of God is entering into you to bring about the purification of Soul.

Sometimes people have experiences with the Light and Sound before coming to ECK, but they don't know what

159

it all means. The Light and Sound are actual, definite aspects of the Holy Spirit, understood and achieved through the Spiritual Exercises of ECK. Some of these are given in books such as *ECKANKAR—The Key to Secret Worlds* and *The Spiritual Notebook*. The ECK teachings are built specifically upon these two pillars of God in a direct, knowable way.

Usually we are introduced to the inner teachings in the dream state or through Soul Travel. But these experiences are merely rungs on the ladder to God. That's all. They are not sacred in themselves.

We begin in the dream state by looking through the veils of illusion, where many things appear in symbols and distortions. But as we go further along in ECK, the distortions are put aside and we see more clearly. First it's through a glass, darkly; and then face-to-face. Though not generally understood by those who read the Bible, this process of unfoldment is what Saint Paul referred to.

The Hundredth Monkey

The title of this talk, "The Hundredth Monkey," was taken from a book of the same name by Ken Keyes, Jr. Someone sent me an article which describes the phenomenon presented in the book.

For many years Japanese scientists had been studying a monkey colony on a Japanese island. In 1952, they began to feed the monkeys sweet potatoes dropped in the sand. The monkeys didn't like the taste of the sand, so for a while they ate very carefully around it.

The story is told that an eighteen-month-old monkey named Imo went to the stream one day, washed her sweet potato, and found that it was much easier to eat when it was clean. Imo showed this trick to her mother, who agreed it was a good idea, and also to her young friends. Pretty soon her playmates were washing their sweet potatoes, and they too took this grand idea home to their families. So from 1952 to 1958, all the young monkeys and the parents who imitated them learned to wash the sweet potatoes before eating them. The other adult monkeys, having no one to set an example, kept up the old way and just continued to eat around the sand.

At that point in the story, something interesting happened. Let's say a total of ninety-nine monkeys on the island had learned to wash their sweet potatoes. As soon as the hundredth monkey had joined in and learned the trick, it was like the turning of the key. All at once the rest of the monkeys on the island started to wash their sweet potatoes before eating them.

It's said that the scientists then noticed an even more phenomenal occurrence: Through a sudden jump in consciousness, colonies of monkeys on other islands spontaneously began to wash their sweet potatoes. The author of the story conjectured that once a certain portion of the monkeys learned to do it, the idea was somehow picked up throughout the group entity.

This is the dynamic law referred to in ECK when we say that as one person unfolds, the whole human race is uplifted a little bit. There has already been a noticeable change in consciousness in the years since the teachings of ECK were brought out. Many initiates who have been in ECK for several years have observed that the people just now coming into ECK are farther along than we were when we first joined. For this reason, it would be a good idea to try to learn from the new people as well as teach them. They may have fresh ideas about ECK which even Fourth and Fifth Initiates can benefit from. And once we reach that certain point—the hundredth monkey—another leap in consciousness will take place, and the ECK teachings will naturally reach out to the rest of the world.

Formula Technique

I would like to present a spiritual exercise that will be of help in the dream state and also with Soul Travel. Those of you who wish to try it out can do so later tonight and in the weeks to come. This spiritual exercise, called the Formula technique, was given to me by Peddar Zaskq. It can help you reach any level from the Second to the Fifth Planes.

You may want to go to the second level, the Astral Plane, which corresponds to the emotional body, to find out why there is an emotional bond with another person. The third level, the Causal Plane, is where you find the seed of all karma created in the past and learn about the past lives that influence you today. The Mental Plane is the level where mental processes originate, where inspiration and ideas may be found in whatever field you are interested in. At the top of this fourth level is the Etheric Plane, which corresponds to the subconscious or unconscious attitudes that motivate you. Then comes the Soul Plane, the level of Self-Realization, the first of the true spiritual worlds.

Like so many other ECKists, I used to go into contemplation and then drop off to sleep. I just assumed that my contemplation would carry over into the dream state, like a natural bridge. But so often when I had an experience on the inner planes, I would wonder whether it happened on the Astral, Causal, or Mental Plane.

I couldn't always distinguish the difference. Many of the experiences on the Mental Plane and the Astral Plane, for instance, are similar enough that sometimes you can't tell on which plane they occurred. It would be nice if someone held up a brightly painted sign in the dream state: "You have arrived on the Astral Plane!" But you can't count on it.

The Formula technique is like a visitor's pass to the other planes. It can even be used by a First or Second Initiate to visit the Soul Plane. This spiritual exercise, which takes about fifteen to twenty minutes, is done at bedtime. It's very simple, and it goes with the sound of HU, a holy name for God. This is how it was given to me.

To reach the Second, or Astral, Plane, use Formula Two. First chant HU two times, then breathe deeply two times. Repeat it again—chant HU twice and breathe deeply twice. Then do it again—HU two times, breathe two times. You don't have to set your timer, because all of a sudden you will know that it's time to stop chanting. Then go to bed. If you do the spiritual exercise lying on your back, just roll over, make yourself comfortable, and very gently hold the thought "Formula Two" in mind as you go to sleep.

You needn't worry about it or perform some special ritual, such as lying straight in bed with your toes pointing up to the ceiling and your hands folded on your chest, or anything like that. Just keep "Formula Two" lightly in mind, and drift off to sleep.

If you wake up and remember something that happened on the inner planes, try to write it down right then, because you'll probably forget most of it by morning. Writing these experiences down as soon as they come is a most difficult discipline. But if you can get in the habit, you will find the full spectrum of your life slowly opening to you, like the petals of a flower.

Going to the Third, or Causal, Plane, the plane of seed karma and past lives, is equally simple with Formula Three: Chant HU three times, and breathe deeply three times. Repeat it again—three HU's, three breaths. Keep doing this until you know within that it's time to quit. As you go to sleep, very gently, without becoming locked on it, try to hold the thought, "Formula Three."

You can aim for the Mental Plane by chanting four HU's, taking four deep breaths, and falling asleep with "Formula Four" lightly in mind. To visit the Soul Plane, chant HU five times, breathe five times, and gently think "Formula Five."

And that's all there is to the Formula technique.

When writing the experiences in your dream journal, you will find it helpful to put "Formula Two" (or "Three" or "Four" or "Five") at the top of the page, to indicate what you were trying to achieve that night. Then add the date and write down the experience. Eventually you will develop a feel for which plane you should be working on that particular evening.

Once you have any degree of success with this technique, you will start to see a different texture to the experiences on each plane. Then begin comparing the experiences of each plane. Try to see if there is a thread that runs through them. In one way or another, Soul will try to come through to give you what you need to know for your spiritual unfoldment.

ECKANKAR International Youth Conference, New York, New York, Saturday, April 18, 1987

What we are actually learning in ECK is how to enter into the gift of divine love, and it shows up in so many humble ways.

10

Gas or God?

It can take me a while to decide on titles for my talks. Usually one keeps lighting up in gold. This is how the ECK-Vidya, the Golden-tongued Wisdom, works. I may not be sure, but the ECK wants it a certain way.

Gift of Divine Love

Many ECK initiates find themselves in similar positions—the ECK says to do something a certain way but you're not sure. You have to put your own opinions and feelings to the side and carry it out, especially if it's something that will benefit everyone else. Sometimes I have misgivings, too, wondering if a certain thing is really supposed to happen. In a case like that, I'll check it, then double- and triple-check it. If it's supposed to be done, I'll just go ahead and do it without letting my feelings get into it. Later I'm so grateful to the ECK for seeing that it got done, because I might not have had the strength on my own.

What we are actually learning in ECK is how to enter into the gift of divine love, and it shows up in so many humble ways.

Nubby and Sunshine

At home our neighbors' beautiful black cat, Nubby, began to come over for visits just as my wife was taking our little dog outside for her daily walks. Our squeaky front door is the signal. Every time we open it, here comes the cat. Nubby visited quite a bit when she was new to the neighborhood and shy, but she kept her distance from our dog, Molly.

We don't know Molly's exact age because she was a street dog when we found her. We think she's about fourteen years old. She has been totally deaf for awhile and last summer she lost most of her vision, too. So now she's a bundle of love with an extraordinary sense of smell. Though she sleeps a lot these days, the one thing that can get her moving is the smell of garlic. Whenever food is being prepared with garlic in it, even if she's sound asleep, her nose starts to quiver. She raises her head to sniff the air, then gets up and heads straight to the kitchen. The aroma of the garlic provides her with a trail to follow.

When my wife and Molly would go out for a walk, Nubby would come over, and pretty soon my wife began to pet the cat. My wife is basically a dog person, but somehow Nubby got to her—you know how animals can work their way into your affections. Day after day she came over to get her back scratched and petted and to hear my wife coo at her. "Nubby, you're such a pretty cat, you're so beautiful," she'd say. Though the cat never purred, her pleasure was evident in the way she would lie down and stretch out on the sidewalk, asking for more.

One day Nubby heard the door squeak open and, as usual, came hurrying over. This time she was carrying something in her mouth. She dropped the object on the lawn, nudged it toward my wife with her nose, then glanced

168

up with a look that said, "This is for you." It was a smooth, white pebble. My wife knew that this special little treasure was Nubby's way of saying thank you. "Why, Nubby, what a beautiful gift," my wife said. "Thank you so much." Nubby, of course, just swelled up with pride.

Weeks passed, it snowed a little bit, and we forgot about the pebble. When the snow melted, we discovered that the little white pebble was still there. Nubby would come over and nuzzle it every so often, just to make sure it was OK.

Nubby has a housemate named Sunshine—Sunny for short. He's a big orange cat that looks like Garfield. Because he is so hefty, his stomach sways from side to side as he waddles along the sidewalk.

Levels of Love

Even though Sunny is very shy and standoffish, he was jealous of the fact that Nubby got all the petting. Eventually he worked up the nerve to come over and allow his fur to be stroked, but only a little bit and then he'd run off.

One day when my wife took Molly outside for a walk, I looked out the window and saw her petting Sunny. When she was finished, I happened to notice that Sunny had a very peculiar expression on his face that I couldn't quite figure out. Later I mentioned to my wife, "Sunny has started to get an odd look on his face. I wonder why."

"He's in love," she said, and I realized it was true. I hadn't thought Sunshine had any love in him at all before this, but gradually he has started to soften up. Unfortunately, his first love was based on jealousy. But even though this isn't the best kind of love, it's better than nothing.

After a while he got more competitive. As soon as our door opened, he'd race over ahead of Nubby to get petted,

169

then turn around and shoot her a warning look: Stay back! I got here first! And Nubby, being a sleek, dignified, feminine cat filled with pure love, knew she wouldn't stand a chance in a fight with big, muscular Sunny.

One time Nubby came tearing down the street, running as fast as she could, with Sunny hot on her heels. Suddenly she dropped flat to the ground and did a funny flip that reminded me of something I saw once when watching championship swimmers on TV. The move was so unexpected that Sunny went flying on past and couldn't stop. In the meantime, Nubby came out of the flip, ran off in the opposite direction, and made a mad dash for my wife, where she knew she'd be safe.

These two cats demonstrate the different levels of love that Soul goes through. First there is no love at all, then Soul experiences a low form of love often driven by anger, jealousy, and spite.

But as we go through different life experiences, we begin to recognize that we can't live with this sort of lower love. Gradually the jealousy goes away, and at some point we realize that the only kind of love worth anything at all is pure love. When we can see this pure love as divine love, we come to know that there is enough for everyone, for all creatures and all things.

Are You God, Too?

Someone gave me an article from the *Catholic Digest* that tells the story of a little boy who lost a tooth while eating candy at a county fair. Naturally he saved it, knowing the tooth fairy would replace it with money.

"I'm going to put this tooth under my pillow," he announced to his parents that night. Since he was eight years old now, his mother figured it was time to tell him the facts of life.

"Do you really think it's necessary anymore?" she asked him. She was trying to find out how much he knew.

"I don't know," he said. But he had a feeling he knew what was coming.

"Who do you think the tooth fairy is?" she asked.

He thought for a minute before answering. Then he said, "You and Dad?" It was a wild guess, but he had suspected it for a while now.

"That's right," she said.

"What about the Easter bunny and Santa Claus?"

"That's us, too," she admitted.

"I wondered how you always knew where the Easter eggs were hidden," he said. "But will I keep getting Christmas presents?"

"You will," his mother assured him. That made him feel a little better. Then she cautioned him, "But don't go telling the younger kids in the neighborhood about this."

The boy started to leave the room. Suddenly he stopped and said, "Oh, no!" Turning to his mother with a worried look on his face, he said, "Are you God, too?"

Parents like to think they are doing children a favor by telling them all these stories. But the day of disillusionment always comes. Faith is lost not only in the trail of myths on which they based their faith, but in their parents as well. Suddenly the kids learn that the people they admired the most have been lying to them. Parents rarely make the connection, but that's when children start to question everything they've been told.

Strange Teachings

At one time I belonged to a church that believed in the resurrection of the body after death. Even as a child I had

171

problems with that one. For instance, I tried to imagine how it would work out with a person who had been chewed up by a whale, digested, released into the ocean where the remains were eaten by other fish, who were then caught and eaten by other people, and so on. When God came on the final day to raise the dead, wouldn't that person be a real mess? But I didn't dare question it out loud.

I tried to believe all these things simply because they were told to me by people I trusted. But even when they quoted scriptures that were supposed to explain why it was so, the idea still didn't make sense. Later, I learned that other religions didn't hold as strictly to this interpretation as did my church, and that many different beliefs have sprung from the same Bible.

These are just some of the stages we go through in our spiritual growth. Finally we realize that truth is never contained in a book, it's contained in the heart. But often the heart of an individual is covered by so many layers that it takes lifetimes to get through them and come to the true nature of Soul.

As one nears the nature of Soul, he comes closer to the nature of truth; the two go together. Then these two unknown ingredients—truth and Soul—which before were based on faith and belief, become based on knowledge and experience. The veils of illusion fall away. The individual then begins to see the essential parts of the teachings of ECK, such as the Light and Sound and the SUGMAD, in the true light.

The Old-fashioned Nutritionist

The Golden-tongued Wisdom, which I mentioned earlier, works in a number of different ways. A few months ago I felt my body undergoing another change, so I decided

172

to try a different nutritionist. Health and nutrition can be a full-time endeavor if you really want to get into it on your own. As soon as you find a system or diet that works, your body changes again and you have to start all over. I find it much easier to just go to a nutrition specialist, hear what he has to say, select the parts that make sense, and reject the rest.

I made an appointment with a nutritionist that someone had recommended to me. The address turned out to be on an obscure, winding back street with no easy access from the freeway. Immediately the Golden-tongued Wisdom flashed out an early warning: This is not the mainstream. But since I was there anyway, I decided to see it through.

I finally figured out how to get to the parking lot behind the rundown building; then I went inside and climbed the stairs to his office. The shabby condition of the walls and rooms offered another indication of what this man had to offer. I was paying attention. Before I even sat down, he handed me a clipboard with a lengthy questionnaire that took almost fifteen minutes to fill out.

"How long have you been in practice?" I asked him.

"About eight years," he said with a bitter laugh. His attitude gave me pause, too.

After we'd chatted a while, I asked him to describe the nutrition program he would recommend. As he began to rattle off his agenda, I suddenly got an eerie, clammy feeling. These were methods I had gone through about ten years ago, right up to the point where they were doing more harm than good, and eventually I had to drop them.

Not wanting to hurt his feelings, I bought some vitamins and promised to call in a week to let him know whether or not I wanted to continue with his program. It seemed only fair to at least give it some consideration.

It was already dark that late wintry afternoon when I left his office, so I got in my car and turned on the lights.

Getting out of the place proved even more difficult than getting in. I drove around the parking lot until I found the exit, which brought me out to a narrow alley. This I followed until I came to a four-lane street. Seeing no signs, I decided to turn left, that being the direction I had come from. There was no other traffic in sight.

I had driven only a short distance when a strange scene appeared before me. A huge bank of headlights, spread across the entire width of the four-lane street, was moving toward me.

A sudden feeling of warmth surged through me, the kind that accompanies a startling realization: I was traveling the wrong way down a one-way street! The mass of cars ahead must have been waiting at a traffic signal a couple of blocks away. I quickly jerked the steering wheel to the right, felt the car bounce up over the curb, and ended up on somebody's lawn.

I sat there in a sweat, wondering how I could have missed the one-way sign. As soon as the traffic passed, I did a neat U-turn and got back onto the street—in the right direction this time.

I realized that the ECK-Vidya, the Golden-tongued Wisdom, had spoken once again. It was saying: This doctor's treatment is the wrong way to go; it will take you backward. If you proceed along this route, you'll end up in a lot of trouble.

Then, just out of curiosity, I drove back to the alley and found that there was no sign.

You have to pay attention when something occurs in your daily life which seems so out of character that it makes you question how it happened or whether you missed a step somewhere. Often you'll find that you didn't miss a step at all. The incident was simply the ECK's way of trying to get a message through to you about something else. The hints can be so subtle that most people overlook them and never make the connection. But if you are open to the Holy Spirit, you might see an indication of the future course that you should chart for yourself in order to avoid problems.

When the week was up, I called the nutritionist to let him know that I had decided not to try his program at this time. I was very nice about it, of course. Just because his methods aren't for me doesn't mean they won't prove helpful to someone else. There is a level of treatment for every level of consciousness, just as there are different religions to fit the various states of consciousness.

Looking at Yourself

It doesn't pay to be critical of others. An ECK initiate learned this lesson after pointing out to a friend of hers, "I don't think you realize how often you say 'you know' in the course of a conversation." He was taken aback. "No, I didn't realize it," he admitted. But he graciously thanked her for mentioning it and promised to do better in the future.

The phone was ringing as she walked in her door. She quickly picked up the receiver and chatted with the caller for several minutes. Then she went to another room to pick up the messages on her answering machine and discovered that part of her conversation had been recorded. As she played it back, she was amazed to hear herself saying "you know" after every few words. Remembering how she had corrected her friend for the very same thing, she was quite embarrassed.

Often we see in others the faults which are nearest to us. If you catch yourself criticizing someone else, stop. Take a moment to look at yourself and ask, in a gentle, noncritical way, Is it myself I'm seeing in this person?

Many times you'll find that the weaknesses you notice in others are really your own. This awareness, which comes with the expansion of consciousness, can save a lot of grief. It can smooth out many kinks on the road back to God.

Gas or God?

One evening a Higher Initiate was driving home from an ECK Satsang class. He felt pretty good as he drove the winding stretch of road that would take him the remaining fifty-seven miles.

About halfway home he happened to glance at the gas gauge. Uh-oh—the needle was on empty. He had forgotten to check it before he left home. Now he started to worry. He still had about thirty miles to go on this dark, deserted road. What if he ran out of gas before he got home?

I know what I can do, he thought. I'll chant HU!

What was his purpose in chanting? To give him enough gas to get home, of course. The empty tank was his own oversight, but why go through any inconvenience if he didn't have to?

Over and over he chanted HU, trying to maintain high hopes that the ECK would get him out of this fix. If he just kept chanting, maybe he could make it all the way home.

Suddenly an inner voice broke through the HU, interrupting his thoughts. It said, "Do you want gas or God?"

We often chant HU when we are in trouble, but that should never overshadow its true function. It isn't meant to fill gas tanks, heal broken bones, or get us an A on a test we haven't studied for. We should never lose sight of the fact that HU is the holy name of God. Its purpose is to draw us closer, in our state of consciousness, to the Divine Being.

"OK, I understand," the Higher Initiate said out loud. Once he got the point, he was able to totally surrender to the situation he had set in motion, and realize that even if he ran out of gas, the problem was not insurmountable.

The lesson he learned was invaluable; even more so because it came at a time when he was right near the edge, anxious and afraid. We are usually more alert, aware, and alive at that point where we fear for our survival than when we are happy and contented.

He did make it home, by the way.

Wind Chimes

The protection of the ECK works in many ways. A woman told me about an experience she had one Saturday when she went to the office to get caught up on some work. Her husband dropped her off in front of the building, and they agreed that he would come back at a certain time to take her home.

No one else was in the office that day, so she got right to work. When it looked like she would finish up sooner than she expected, she decided to call her husband and have him come early. But when she picked up the phone, the line was dead. She tried the phones in the other offices, too—all dead. The silence made her very nervous.

Then her imagination went to work. What if an intruder had broken into the building and cut the phone wires? Should she try to run out the front door? No, she didn't dare—he could be lurking in some corner, just waiting for her to leave. And with the phone lines dead, she couldn't call for help. What should she do? The more she thought about it, the more panicky she got.

The best bet was to stay in her office and try to keep busy until her husband arrived. She sat down at her desk, put her attention on the Mahanta, and got back to work.

Pretty soon she heard a familiar sound, like the melodious tinkling of chimes in the wind. She and her husband had a beautiful set of wind chimes on their porch, and the soft music was very comforting. She got so absorbed in what she was doing that she actually thought she was at home. In fact, when her husband came to get her a little while later, she looked up and was surprised to find herself still at the office.

She realized that the music of the chimes, which brought such comfort, was merely an indication of the Sound Current, which is the ECK, or Holy Spirit. It came to say, "Don't worry, the protection of the Master is here with you. Go ahead and finish your work; everything is all right."

Invisible Protection

There are times when people are rendered invisible for their protection, and this may very likely have happened with this initiate. When she heard the chimes and thought she was at home, she was home; and if anyone had walked past the office, they would not have seen her.

The ECK sometimes comes through and makes me invisible to others, too. Occasionally even close friends will walk right past me, an arm's length away, and not even notice me. I can see them, but they can't see me. For one reason or another, at that particular time, the ECK had changed my vibrations and theirs, putting us on different wavelengths. Other ECKists have had this experience, too; it occurs more often than people realize.

Meeting Paul Twitchell

In 1974, a GI stationed at a military base began to have out-of-body experiences while in the barracks. Sometimes he rose up out of his physical body and went soaring through the ceiling. Other times he had no sense of movement but was able to see through walls, lockers, and other solid objects. He thought these experiences were so fantastic that he wrote each one down so he wouldn't forget.

On August 9, 1974, during one of the experiences, he met a man whose face he knew he'd never forget. He described the man's body as sparkling like a million stars— which is how the Astral body appears.

About ten years later, while browsing in a bookstore, he saw the book, *ECKANKAR—The Key to Secret Worlds* and had a strong urge to buy it. He took it home but didn't actually get around to reading it for some time. One night at bedtime he picked it up and started flipping through the pages. Then he turned it over to look at the back cover—and just about dropped the book in shock. There he saw a picture of Paul Twitchell and immediately recognized him as the spiritual traveler he had seen in the starry body ten years earlier. At this point, he said, he knew that ECKANKAR was what he had been looking for.

Although these incidents aren't common, frequently enough we do hear about people who had experiences with the ECK Masters long before they read or heard anything about ECKANKAR here on the physical plane.

The consciousness in general has been elevated in the last twenty years or so, to the point where most people are now familiar with the concept of out-of-body travel, even if they don't really believe in it. Through the work of authors like Shirley MacLaine and others, the idea of having experiences beyond the physical body has become more acceptable.

Brought Back to Life

Recently my wife and I overheard a conversation between two elderly gentlemen who were seated in the booth next to us in a restaurant in Chanhassen, Minnesota. One man mentioned that his wife had died recently. The other man then began telling him about the time he'd suffered a heart attack and was rushed to the VA hospital. Before the doctors were able to bring him around, he had a near-death experience that took him to an incredibly beautiful place. Shock treatments were administered in an effort to resuscitate him, and suddenly he found himself being pulled back to the physical body. He was so disappointed that, upon coming awake, he shouted out in anger. Naturally this reaction came as quite a surprise to his doctors. Where was this man's gratitude? After all, they had brought him back to life.

We don't know if the man who had lost his wife grasped the significance of his friend's story, but maybe it offered him some reassurance of life after death.

When the two gentlemen got up to leave, the widower went ahead to pay the bill while the storyteller lingered behind to leave a tip.

"Excuse me," I said as he went past our booth. "My wife and I couldn't help overhearing your story. We found it very interesting. It sounds like a wonderful experience."

He wasn't the least bit embarrassed or offended by our eavesdropping; in fact, he seemed eager to talk about it some more. "Yes," he said, "I died and went to heaven, and then I came back. Now I'm no longer afraid of death. On the other hand, I take better care of myself than I used to, and I think it's because I'm no longer afraid to live."

We chatted for a few minutes more, and then he left. As I looked out the window and watched him get into the car with his friend, it occurred to me that at some point this man would be introduced to ECKANKAR. His location in Chanhassen almost assures it. And someday, when the time is right, he will make a connection between his experience and our meeting.

How Soul Finds Freedom

Contact with the other worlds helps one lose the fear of death, and that removes the fear of living here and now, today. This is what we offer in ECKANKAR, by showing people how to have a conscious awareness of experiences on the other planes, both in the dream state and through Soul Travel.

I am trying to present the teachings of ECK as simply and clearly as possible to those who sincerely want a greater awareness of their true Self through the expanded consciousness. One day we must each give up the small self—and I don't mean the body—to become a Co-worker with God. Even now while we are still living in the human body, we must share with others the message of the Light and Sound. Only through this awareness can Soul find freedom, now or ever.

ECKANKAR International Youth Conference, New York, New York, Sunday, April 19, 1987

She didn't realize that the sounds of different musical instruments are just some of the ways the ECK, which is the Voice of God, speaks to people.

11

God Is Speaking through You

Always on my mind is how to speak about ECK, the Holy Spirit, in such a way that those with no background in the ECK teachings can understand how the SUGMAD, or God, works through the ECK in our everyday lives.

Inner Music

Some years ago, before the teachings of ECK were again brought out to the public, a woman began hearing musical sounds. Since she didn't know what to make of it, she decided to consult her priest.

"What is this music that I keep hearing?" she asked.

"Well, you're an artist, and artistic people sometimes hear and see unusual things," he said. "But it's really not normal." He then recommended that she seek professional help. "Therapy will help you overcome this condition," he said.

Following his advice, she made an appointment with a therapist to discuss her problem.

"What seems to be the matter?" he asked.

"Lately I've been hearing this beautiful music playing,"

she explained. "It makes me feel very good, but I just don't know what it is. It never happened before."

She didn't realize that the sounds of different musical instruments are just a few of the ways the ECK, which is the Voice of God, speaks to people.

The doctor figured she was suffering from some deep-seated psychosis. "You'll need hypnosis to get to the bottom of this," he said gravely.

The woman thought that the priest and the therapist were wrong to treat this as a complaint. The music she heard was uplifting; it seemed to heal and comfort her. She only wanted to understand why it was happening, not get rid of it.

She decided the easiest way to get through the session was to fake it, so when the doctor commenced his routine to hypnotize her, she played along.

"I feel better now," she assured him at the end of the session. He was very pleased that his treatment was such a success. She thanked him profusely for his help and never went back.

Several years passed, and her experiences continued. Then, in 1969, she came across the book *In My Soul I Am Free,* the story of Paul Twitchell and ECKANKAR. For the first time, she found an explanation for the inner music. The book told about the Sound Current of ECK, more commonly known as the Holy Spirit or the Voice of God, which can be heard as various sounds and sometimes seen as light.

A few days later in another bookstore she saw *The Tiger's Fang,* in which Paul tells of his spiritual journey into the other worlds. She read with fascination his descriptions of the many manifestations of the Sound and Light, and meetings with the gods of the different planes.

She knew now that somewhere there were other people

who could help her understand what she was going through. She didn't know where they were, but she had a feeling that they were almost within reach.

Not long after that she saw a notice about an introductory talk on ECKANKAR and immediately made plans to attend. As soon as she walked into the room, she recognized that these were the teachings she'd had inner contact with these last few months. She listened to a discussion of the different aspects of ECK, and she knew that this was where she belonged.

God in Expression

As we go about our day, ideas come through on how to solve problems, how to make our work easier, or how to make things better for someone else. These ideas come from the creative imagination which, to state it as simply as possible, is God in expression, manifesting Its creation in this world through our actions. This is God speaking through us. The creative imagination is the element that makes us godlike.

By keeping his attention on the ECK, the ECKist is uplifted and spiritualized, so that his interactions with his family, friends, and neighbors ideally are of the highest nature. I say "ideally," but it's not always practically so, for the road to God-Realization is long and hard. We are constantly being tested to see if, when we face truth, we are found worthy of receiving it.

Renovated Restaurant

I went to a seafood restaurant that had recently been remodeled. Everything was brand new. For years it had been a dark, dreary place with fishnets hanging from the walls. Every time you walked in, you felt like you were entering the lower decks of a revolutionary-war battleship for a meal of hardtack and water. The atmosphere wasn't uplifting at all.

Now not only was it tastefully decorated, but somebody had been very practical in selecting the new fixtures and color scheme. The booth seats were covered with a durable plastic to protect against scuff marks from children's shoes, and the seat backs were in a plaid design with shades of gravy brown and French-dressing orange — perfect for hiding greasy fingerprints. The carpeting had a gray-green-brown pattern with little red flecks, so that spilled-ketchup stains would fit right in. The tables were clean and shining, no longer encumbered with the tablecloths they used to have.

"Somebody put a lot of thought into renovating this restaurant," I commented to the waitress who brought the water. "There isn't much you can throw around in here that's going to be noticed. And yet it looks bright and pretty and easy to clean."

"That's right," she agreed. "This restaurant now belongs to a chain. Everything was tested out in another location before it was incorporated here, and these features were found to be the very best."

It occurred to me that this is how the Master works with the spiritual student. Without realizing it, the student is tested in every area of his life to see how he handles the stresses of living. This is to make sure that when truth is put upon his shoulders, he will be strong enough to carry it.

Gaining Spiritual Strength

Many years ago I read the story of Milo of Crotona, who became known as the strongest man in his country.

He began to build his strength by walking the streets of ancient Greece with a baby calf perched on his back. With each passing day the animal grew a little bit bigger, a little bit heavier. But because Milo kept up the practice every day, he barely noticed it. His strength increased proportionately, so that at no point was the weight too much for him to carry. By the time the calf grew into a full-size bull, Milo was acknowledged as the strongest man in Crotona.

This, in effect, is how the Mahanta helps the student of ECK to build strength. It starts with a little bit of truth given each day, like carrying a baby calf. Then you get a little bit more and a little bit more. As you move on in the initiations of ECK, you grow increasingly stronger, until finally your spiritual strength becomes more than anyone could imagine.

Milo liked to challenge the other men by closing his hand around a pomegranate and daring anyone to take it from him. The others would try to pry his hand open, squeezing and pulling on his fingers with all their might. Only when they finally gave up would he release his grip. He'd hold out his hand to display an unbruised pomegranate. This feat not only proved his great strength, but also his ability to control it.

Spiritual strength is not the kind that needs to be shown off; one can be gentle or weak in the body yet strong in Spirit.

Call of Soul

As the saying goes: As above, so below. Above being somewhere in the inner worlds where the spiritual travelers move and have their being, and below being here on earth. Many of the Higher Initiates are conscious of going into the other worlds, sometimes to the Temples of Golden

Wisdom. They help and work with people who know nothing about ECK here on the physical plane.

Traveling to these other planes in the Soul body, the Higher Initiates acquaint the individual with just enough truth for a little bit to trickle down to the human consciousness and into his everyday life. Then, as the person grows spiritually stronger, the call of Soul becomes stronger.

Finally the day comes when the jump is made. Through some source in his outer life, whether a book or another person or whatever, he comes across ECKANKAR and recognizes that this is what he has been looking for. At last he has found a teaching which explains, for the first time, the Sound and Light, their relation to God, and what they mean to him as an individual.

At the point where the inner and outer realities of the seeker are merged into one, his search for truth is well on its way. Now he will learn to move into the higher worlds of the Holy Spirit where he has never been able to travel before. He is on his way to becoming a Co-worker with God.

Where Are the Miracles?

Recently a minister who had taken a look at the teachings of ECKANKAR said to an ECK initiate, "Where are the miracles? I don't see any mention of miracles in ECK. Does anybody walk on water or fly in the air?"

"Bugs can walk on water and birds can fly in the air," the ECKist said. "The real miracle is the man who can walk with God every day." His answer well expresses the indefinable godlike state of consciousness which I am trying to release in those who really care.

Miracles in ECK happen all the time—the miracles of healing or of understanding, miracles which occur through prophecies, and so on. But I purposely avoid talking much about them, because it can leave a person too dependent on an outer authority. This is not our goal in ECKANKAR.

Phenomenal miracles were a big thing two thousand years ago. Even today they are still part of the belief system in developing countries where modern science doesn't have such a hold over the mind. The people have a very simple, firm belief that there is a power stronger than they are, which can help them out of their troubles. And because of the strength of their belief, they project this power to anyone who has even the smallest amount of healing ability, thereby compounding the power of the healer. Where there is no dependence upon reason or scientific explanations, superstition thrives. This provides ripe ground for miracles to occur.

Asking for Help

So many spiritual healings take place today, but all too often they go unrecognized. Since a person is usually seeing a doctor for his ailment at the same time he's asking the ECK for help, he credits the medical treatment for his cure.

Recently an individual's initial tests and X rays indicated that he had a malignant condition. So he asked for help from the ECK. When he went back to the doctor, subsequent tests revealed the condition to be a benign cyst. Naturally his doctor wondered how the initial tests and X rays could have been so wrong.

What happened, of course, was that the whole nature of the illness was changed into something curable. With a simple treatment or medication for the lesser ailment, the patient went away very satisfied that it was the doctor who had healed him. So what can you say?

It isn't that the miracles are fewer today than they used to be, but that scientific techniques obscure the miraculous nature of the healings. In an affluent society, the climate of skepticism is too strong to allow for a belief in miracles. This is why, when they do occur, there are very few who recognize them. Very few understand that the healing is from the ECK, from the spiritual power. But even if a miracle is given, keep in mind that it won't last forever. Even the people that Jesus healed eventually died.

The ECK doesn't only use science to heal. It uses whatever is available. After all, the creative mind of man is imbued with Spirit, especially when it is trying to create something for the good of mankind. This includes medicine, of course. It has become a very necessary part of our society. For this reason, when people ask what to do about a certain illness, I generally tell them to go see a doctor.

In more instances than I can name, it is not past karma that has caused the illness, as so many people would like to believe. Many physical ailments are simply a product of the times. Nuclear weapons exploded into the atmosphere since World War II have changed the very air we breathe. Increased food production has led to the necessity to preserve it for a longer shelf life, which means we now routinely consume a variety of preservatives. It's a catch-22 situation: Science has been able to improve the quality of life faster than our bodies have been able to evolve.

Opening the Heart

The creative power of ECK doesn't work only through ECKists. It also works through musicians, healers, writers, homemakers, and businessmen. It works everywhere, and it works best through those who love what they are doing. If you are in a line of work you enjoy or in a marriage filled with love, you will find that you are many times more creative than a person who is unhappy.

Some of the songs played at ECK seminars are so beautiful; you can actually feel the creative current, the Holy Spirit, coming through. In time the music of ECK will fall into all of the traditional categories, such as folk and classical, but it will still be a different kind of music.

One of the ECK musicians gave me an audiocassette with samples of his compositions. He wanted to know if it was any good, and if not, how it could be changed to better reflect the ECK.

I listened to the entire tape. It was all good; but one piece in particular had a special quality: it opened the heart. There was nothing wrong with the rest of the music—it was very good, too—but it lacked that certain quality.

No matter what classification it falls into, I'm drawn to music that opens my heart. This piece was inspired by the ECK working through the individual. At the time it was written, he was very close to the Holy Spirit. That's what made it so special.

Everyday Joy

Closeness to the Holy Spirit allows the creative current to come through. And as we release our creative abilities, we achieve the upliftment of the spiritual consciousness.

These abilities are not something that can be taught in a workshop. The ECK works through the heart, not the head. When we try to accomplish the creative principles through logic and reasoning, or by writing them down and memorizing them, it doesn't work. So the Mahanta, the Living ECK Master tries to open an individual's heart to the Holy Spirit.

Once this happens, the revelations begin; the person now finds joy in everyday things. When he is at the point where he can find joy in even one or two things, gradually his life begins to expand. There are hardships, too, and life doesn't always go the way he expects, so sometimes the music flows out from heartache. But even at this stage of his creativity, he is in the process of becoming godlike. And the ultimate state of being godlike is God-Realization.

Visits to Inner Temples

We are moving into a golden age of spirituality. As we come to the end of the twentieth century, the creative fountain is being opened, and many more people will be able to manifest that which is of the higher worlds. Often the preparation or training for this creative flow takes place in the Temples of Golden Wisdom.

There are several Temples of Golden Wisdom in the lower worlds, including the Katsupari Monastery and the temple at Agam Des here on the Physical Plane, as well as those on the Astral, Causal, Mental, and Etheric planes. The ECK writings generally mention the main Temple of Golden Wisdom on each plane, but there are numerous minor temples, too.

In the dream state or during Soul Travel, the seeker is accompanied to one of the temples by an ECK Master, such as Rebazar Tarzs, Peddar Zaskq, or Wah Z. There the seeker can read from one of the books of the Shariyat-Ki-Sugmad. This is part of the ECK path. There are two volumes of the Shariyat in print here on earth, but many more are kept in the other temples on the inner planes.

Sometimes the human mind cannot contain what the individual takes in while traveling in the Soul body. But even if he doesn't remember what he has read, the golden truth is within him.

Though the temples on the lower planes are usually located in a building of some kind, on the Soul Plane and higher there is no such structure. Here you find the action of the Sound and the Light working directly with you as Soul, coming into you to uplift and give the knowledge and wisdom to which your state of consciousness entitles you. Here it is impossible to speak of what you take in, because there simply are no words for it.

Following the Law of Silence

The ECK teachings remind us of the Law of Silence. If you attempt to put your experience into words, it can cause problems with those around you who do not believe you are speaking the truth. In their doubt, they will do everything they can to destroy it for you.

Truth is given to each individual in a way that he can understand, and it is just for that person. Sometimes one is given a little bit of truth on one of the lower worlds of the Astral Plane just to see what he will do with it. And what he'll do with it is often so predictable that you wonder why the spiritual travelers even bothered giving it to him.

He'll wake up and run to tell the nearest person: "God spoke to me last night!" The responses are usually pretty predictable, too, ranging from, "You'd better be quiet about that," to "Eat your breakfast and go to work," to "Keep cool—you'll be OK in a day or two."

Generally the person who sees one of the minor gods on the inner planes thinks he has met the highest deity, for this being is far more luminous than he ever could have imagined. When the human consciousness is dim, you could put the person next to a lightning bug and the person would be impressed. In extreme cases, he's so certain he has met the ultimate deity that he wants to give up his family and his job, go out and start a religion, and find followers to carry this message to all of mankind. So he goes out there and babbles the news, and then wonders why he's considered strange.

Show Time

In planning for future ECK seminars, I'm trying to find new ways to bring forth the expression of the Holy Spirit. We are gradually expanding the music program, but I would also like to see the teachings of ECK expressed through other formats, such as plays. This should open up a whole new area of creativity through which the message of the Holy Spirit can flow.

I sent out a blanket invitation for play ideas. Then we put out a call for playwrights among the initiates who might want to work on a script for this project. This is a specialized area of writing. It requires the ability to convert the ECK message into a visual as well as verbal presentation, and make it entertaining for the audience.

I didn't suggest a topic or say how long it should be; in fact, there were no guidelines at all. Given such complete freedom, most people sat right down, thought about it for a while, and couldn't come up with anything.

Finally I sent out a more specific request: Can you write a play based on the chapter "Show Time" from *In the Company of ECK Masters* by Phil Morimitsu? This chapter contains sensitive material. It presents a different angle on karma and responsibility than most of us learned

194

in Christianity. In a humorous way, the author confronts the Christian belief regarding the justification of sins by faith. Many people like to believe you can live like a complete rake until the eleventh hour, let's say 11:56 p.m., but as long as you repent at the last minute and accept Jesus before you die, you'll go to heaven.

Show Time offers a different perspective on the whole issue of responsibility for the transgressions we commit against each other and how Jesus fits into the picture. It shows that at some point we have to take responsibility for our own actions, then go on from there.

I'm sensitive to this approach because many people's beliefs are founded in Christianity, and it's very good for them. Yet, there are also others who have outgrown what they were taught in the church of their upbringing. Now they are just waiting for someone to come along and put before them a truth which they can recognize for themselves, such as the principles of karma and self-responsibility.

A part-time scriptwriter who received an invitation to work on *Show Time* was a bit concerned. His wife, a Christian, became noticeably upset that he would write about such a thing. I could understand her feelings; but the fact is, when truth comes out, it's going to step on somebody's toes. Even Jesus stepped on some toes, in that his teachings went against the practices of the Jewish people.

We don't want to be in the position of invalidating or ignoring the beliefs of others. For this reason, I often include stories and principles that relate to a religion people are familiar with. If they are strong in their religion, it will give them more to build on. But if their belief in their religion is floundering because they have outgrown it, it can open the door to ECKANKAR, where perhaps they can find teachings that make more sense to them.

The scriptwriter decided that he couldn't work on *Show Time* because it offended his wife. But maybe he could come up with an idea for a future ECK play.

Out of the Blue

In the meantime, on his regular job he was asked to participate in a project to renovate a sixty-year-old building. "We want to do a complete face-lift on it," his boss said. "Let's come up with a whole new color scheme."

His first step was to take several black-and-white photographs of the building. Then he planned to call a few art-supply stores and try to find a particular brand of dye. The idea was to paint each picture a different color so his boss could see what the finished product would look like and make his choice.

A couple of days later he still hadn't found the right dyes to complete the assignment. His boss called him into his office and began to chew him out for not moving fast enough. When the meeting showed no signs of ending soon, he figured the best way to get through it was to let his mind wander until his boss ran out of steam.

He thought over some of the remarks his wife had made about the ECK play. This reminded him of an introductory lecture he had attended at one of the colleges, and he began to mentally review some of the questions the students had asked at the end of the talk. There seemed to be a thread of some kind running through his thoughts, but he couldn't quite make the connection. Maybe an idea for a play was trying to come through. He couldn't wait for the meeting to end so he could get home and work on it.

Before he left the office, his boss reminded him once again that the project had to be completed by a certain date. Then his wife called and gave him a list of groceries to pick up on his way home. His idea for the play would have to wait.

Following up on some leads, he drove downtown to two art-supply stores. The first place had the wrong brand, and the second had dyes so old that the labels were peeling off the jars. He traveled through several suburbs to get to a third store only to find that they didn't have what he wanted either. Disappointed, he got back in his car and decided to call it a day. As he followed the crawling rush-hour traffic out of town, he suddenly realized he was completely lost. So far, this had not been one of his better days.

Up ahead he noticed a grubby-looking little art store, the kind of place he normally wouldn't bother to patronize. An empty parking space was right in front, and suddenly he got the feeling that the ECK was steering him to it. He quickly pulled over to the curb, parked his car, and went inside.

"We have just what you're looking for," the clerk said, "and we carry it in forty different colors." Delighted to find that they came in handy little bottles, the ECKist took one each of all forty colors. He was so relieved to find what he wanted that he bought a whole bunch of other supplies, too, and left the store with an armload of packages.

Right next door was a hamburger stand. Realizing that he was hungry, he went over and got something to eat. The rush-hour traffic had cleared by then, and it didn't take him long to find a familiar street. He felt pretty satisfied with himself as he headed for home. He found a supermarket and went in to buy some groceries, then stopped at a video store to browse, and decided to rent a movie. All he wanted to do now was go home, kick off his shoes, take a shower, then relax and watch the movie.

It was dark and raining pretty hard as he pulled up in front of his house. There were more than enough packages for two trips, but he decided to save time by carrying everything in at once. With various paper bags full of dyes, art supplies, and groceries clutched precariously in both arms and hands, he started up the front walk.

About halfway to the house, he lost his grip on one of the bags. He heard a strange tinkling sound as it landed on the cement. "Oh, no," he groaned. "I must have broken the bottles of dye." He carefully set the other packages down and reached into the fallen bag to assess the damage.

Thus began an interesting chain of events.

Just as he pulled his hand from the bag, his dog came dashing down the walk to greet him and sniff at the groceries. He scooted the dog away, dismayed to see that his hand was darkened with dye. Worse yet, some of it had managed to drip onto his coat, shirt, and trousers. But no time to worry about that now—he had to take the groceries inside before they got soaked.

"Daddy!" his two little girls yelled gleefully as he walked in the door. Before he could stop them, they ran up and gave him a big hug. But something didn't feel right. Backing away, they noticed some sticky blue stuff on their hands. The younger one immediately reached out to make a hand print on the white wall. "Daddy, look how pretty!" she said. At the same time, the other girl developed an itch on her scalp, which of course she scratched.

He quickly unburdened himself of the bags, groaning some more as he saw the puddle that had formed in the middle of the floor from the dripping dye. Just then his three hungry cats scurried into the room on the way to their food dishes. One cat ran right through the puddle, paused to examine its moist paw, and began to lick it. He sat down briefly in the dye, then ran over and jumped up on the couch.

The man was beside himself. Speechless, he turned away from the mess and stared out the window, only to find that the dye had left a trail of drops up the front steps, which he had tracked into the house. Things couldn't possibly get any worse.

In walked his mother-in-law. She had just come up from the basement with a basket of clean laundry, unaware that anything was wrong. Can you guess where she plunked it down? At this point, he said, you could have fried a hamburger on his head.

He tore open the soggy bag and began going through the bottles in an attempt to get rid of the broken ones. To his surprise, the only one that was cracked was the blue dye. He looked around the room in disbelief, but sure enough, the kids, the cats, and all the stains and streaks were blue.

And then, to use his words, "out of the blue" came the idea for an ECK play. The elusive thread that had escaped him earlier began to form into a full-blown sketch. He envisioned an interview in which one of the ECK Masters would present introductory information about the principles of ECK.

Hurriedly he wiped up the puddle. He knew it would take many hours to thoroughly clean up the mess—but for now he wanted to get started on the play. He worked on it steadily until 2:00 in the morning.

He didn't comment on his wife's reaction when she got home, but he did say the kids needed haircuts, the cats now had blue tongues, and the dog got into the groceries.

The moral of this story is: If you ask to be opened to

the creative flow, one way or another it's going to come through, so it's best to be prepared for everything that comes with it.

ECKANKAR International Creative Arts Festival,
Chicago, Illinois, Friday, June 19, 1987

The elephant couldn't free itself by its own power, nor could its rescuers do it with their strength alone.

12

The Meaning of Surrender

As I was preparing my notes for this talk, I felt waves of heaviness so strong that at times I just wanted to lay down and rest. These are the waves of karma that come from the Souls who attend the ECK seminars. They pass off through the Living ECK Master, the instrument of the ECK, and into the ECK Lifestream.

Shaking off the tiredness, I continued to work on the talk. As other ECK speakers have found, you do the best you can to plan what you're going to say. But often things come up unexpectedly which render the prepared material inappropriate. All you can do is realize that no matter how it comes out, you have to give credit to a higher power, to the ECK, or Holy Spirit.

This is easy enough to do when the talk doesn't turn out well. Then you can say, "It was the will of the ECK." On the other hand, if it turns out well, most of us would say, "*I* sure gave a good talk tonight!"

Like Moving an Elephant

Someone wrote me a letter describing a television show where a young elephant got stuck in a muddy water hole and couldn't get out. The rest of the herd hovered near their companion, obviously wanting to help but having no means to do so. The poor trapped animal was in danger not only from the tigers and other predators that stalk the jungle at night, but also from hunters.

A group of explorers drove by in a jeep and saw the plight of the elephant. They wanted to rescue it, but unfortunately they didn't have the equipment to pull it free. The best they could do was to put a rope around it and somehow prod and encourage it to keep trying to tug its way out of the mud. All the while they spoke soothingly so that it would know they were trying to help. When they finally managed to pull it out, they discovered that it had been caught in a trap placed in the water by poachers.

The elephant couldn't free itself by its own power, nor could its rescuers do it with their strength alone. But once these factors were overcome, the elephant was able to rejoin the herd and return to the freedom of the jungle.

It's the same way with karma, which is the one thing that stands between the individual and surrender. And the lack of surrender is what interferes with one's ability to give and receive love. Karma, surrender, and love — they are all part of the chain.

Coming Full Circle

In ECK we do not lean on justification by faith. This is where, at the last minute, one calls in a minister and says, "I've had a change of heart; I'm gonna go right. Please baptize me so I can go to heaven." On the other hand the biblical phrase, "Whatsoever a man soweth, that also shall he reap," is also too strict in a sense, especially in ECK.

Somebody told me a story that gives a stark example of karma coming around full circle. It was about an individual who started a brutal fight with another man, then walked away and left the other party for dead. His deed never stopped weighing on him, however; he simply could not release his fear of what he had done. Before too long, events formed in such a way that the instruments used for harm in the original attack came back and injured the man who started the fight, so that he died at a young age. The cycle came around very quickly.

It really isn't necessary for it to happen this way. One of the benefits of working with the ECK teachings, of putting your spiritual life in the hands of the Mahanta, is that much of your karma can be worked off in the dream state. So whenever I get letters from people who complain about having bad dreams or nightmares, I'm tempted to write back and ask, "Would you rather have them happen out here in your everyday life?"

Understanding Troubled Waters

Right before the Second Initiation, some people— though not all—may go through a period of troubled waters. They experience upsetting dreams. But the dreams are a lot easier to resolve than conditions out here in the physical. What makes them seem so difficult to bear at the time is the initiate's lack of understanding of the reasons for his problems. I don't usually reply directly to requests for help, because it's better in the long run if a person figures it out for himself. And if they are patient and stay with the spiritual exercises, this period of troubled waters passes.

It isn't that our troubles lessen as we reach the Third, Fourth, and Fifth Initiations; but as we go along in ECK, our understanding becomes greater. When we understand the reason for our suffering, we can bear it more easily. Not only do we begin to see the cause-and effect patterns, but eventually we reach the point where we realize it's best to turn things over to the ECK. We can prevent a lot of karma once we learn to work in a state of detachment, in which all things are done in the name of the Master. In that sense, our life does become easier.

When an individual surrenders to the ECK, he then becomes an instrument for It. This means that no matter where you go or what you do, the ECK uses you as Its vehicle.

One in a Million

A Higher Initiate wrote to an airline to complain about poor service on one of its flights. The airline's response was to reimburse him for $150.00. He was so pleased that he decided to express his gratitude to the airline by using the money to buy two roundtrip tickets. "Anywhere you want to go?" he asked his wife. He was being very grand about it, of course, but at today's fares, $150.00 barely gets two people across the river and back.

"Why don't we go to Florida?" his wife suggested, although $150.00 wouldn't even pay for one ticket that far.

"Let me think about it," he said.

Shortly after that he received a mailing from a company. It offered an all-expenses-paid trip to Florida in exchange for attending a sales pitch on vacation condominiums. The ECKist knew exactly how these condo sales gimmicks worked: All you had to do was contact a salesman, act interested, and you'd get a free trip to view the property. "I think I'll give it a try," he said to his wife.

Fully expecting a high-pressure sales pitch, he steeled himself before entering the agent's office. These people don't give out a free trip without first making you earn it—whether you go or not.

"I came here to inquire about that free trip," he said.

"Well, these are time-lease condos we're selling," the salesman began, "and—"

"Before you go any further," the Higher Initiate said, "I can save you a lot of time. I only came here to find out about the free trip, not to buy anything."

The salesman was bowled over by such honesty. "I guess you don't get to take too many trips," he said.

"Oh, four or five a year," the ECKist admitted.

"That's a lot more than most people take," the salesman said. "How do you manage that?" He was trying to size up this guy.

"I belong to a religious group, and I arrange my work schedule so my wife and I can attend their seminars around the country."

The salesman then went into a very aggressive spiel about the bliss of buying into one of their Florida condos. He used all the usual arm-twisting tactics, certain that somehow the man could be swayed.

"I'm really not interested," the ECKist said each time the salesman paused for breath. He was polite but firm.

It took quite a while before the sales agent was convinced, but finally he had to concede, "I guess this really isn't for you." Then he added, almost to himself, "My boss said there'd be one in a million."

"What do you mean?" the ECKist asked.

"One in a million who can't be sold," the salesman explained. "He already has everything he wants, so you have nothing to offer him."

The salesman suddenly began to talk to the Higher Initiate about more personal matters—his ex-wife, his divorce, and how badly his job was going.

"I used to make a lot of sales until just recently," he explained. "But all of a sudden it stopped, and I haven't been able to sell a thing. I mentioned it to my boss, but all he said was, 'Don't worry about it. Something will come up to help you out of this lull.' "

"The problem is, you're pushing," the Higher Initiate said. "You're trying to sell people on something they don't need. Why not just educate them to the benefits of time-sharing a condo?"

The salesman thought this over. "Now that you mention it, I made more sales when I used to just explain the deal to people, because usually they'd hear something they liked. But lately I've noticed how forcefully the other salesmen pressure customers into buying, and I started doing the same thing."

"Just speak to people with your heart open to them," the Higher Initiate suggested. "Not only will they understand what you're saying, but they'll trust you, because they'll know you are telling them the truth."

"Somebody up there sent you," the salesman said, obviously very impressed with what the Higher Initiate had passed along. He then told him about some of the features of the time-sharing plan, and this time his presentation was relaxed and sincere.

The ECKist found himself listening with growing interest. "Actually, I'd like to take a look at the condo," he said.

"You would?" The salesman was so grateful that he arranged for the ECKist and his wife to get not only the free trip, but a travel bonus that allowed them five nights at a hotel. And before they were finished, he even threw in a free set of luggage.

Family Karma

Karma accounts for those webs and ropes that keep us tied to very old relationships that have been going on for centuries. We are so tied to others by karma before we come into ECK that we cannot make a move without leaning on someone else.

Once we come into ECK, these bands of karma begin to dissolve, and eventually they drop away. Only then can we stand on our own, with love. Our relationships and associations with other people are no longer based on the Law of Karma which says you are thrown together because you have to resolve this or that. Now we have the freedom to choose the people we want around us.

In the 1890s, a young girl crossed the ocean from Europe with her close-knit family of seven. A fever epidemic swept through the ship, and in a matter of days she lost all six brothers and sisters. She arrived in America the only survivor of her family.

She grew up, got married, and had six or seven children of her own. These children, of course, were the siblings she had lost on the ship several years earlier. Only two of them ever married. They had been such a tight karmic group before they left Europe that most of them liked each other's company better than anybody else's.

The hardships they had endured during the ocean crossing were felt even in this lifetime. They all had an unaccountable terror of boarding any kind of ship or boat.

Many of our unexplained fears in this lifetime are based on old karma. Even though we are not conscious of the source of the fear, we react to it anyway.

When one of this woman's grown children was killed in an accident, he reincarnated within four months as the son of his married brother. His parents and other relatives often commented that he had the same personality and mannerisms as his deceased uncle. Even when he grew up, this individual who was now the nephew stayed close to those who had once been his brothers and sisters, doing repairs around their homes and taking care of them just as he had before. To this day, the later generations of this family are still a very tightly knit group.

For people who find their way to ECK, these karmic ties gradually begin to dissolve as they work through the things that have bound them so strongly to each other. Karma of this type is actually a net of fear, and this is what keeps people together through so many lifetimes. But when love comes, fear goes; and with the release of fear comes freedom. This spiritual freedom is what we are looking for in ECK.

Sometimes the karmic debt is too deep to resolve easily. Because of the severity of the trauma that happened in the past, possibly compounded over several lifetimes, it must be worked out very slowly, in its own way. The person may ask for help, but when it comes, he often can't recognize it. In certain cases, the karma is so tightly knotted up that institutionalization may be the only way to give the person's mind and emotions a rest. Then, perhaps, the karmic bonds can begin to unwind.

The Toy Duck

Vanity is often the reason an individual is unable to surrender to the Mahanta and receive divine love.

A photographer told me about a young woman who came to his studio to have her picture taken. He set up the camera and the proper lighting, then had her take a seat against a backdrop of scenery. But when he tried to get her to smile or even just to look pleasant, he had no success. She steadfastly refused to surrender her rigid expression.

Resorting to the techniques he used to make children smile, he brought out an array of toys and gimmicks. Nothing worked. Finally he held up a little rubber duck and squeezed it. The quack-quacks did the trick: In spite of herself, she broke into a beautiful smile. He worked as quickly as possible to capture it on film.

When the negatives were developed, he was pleased to see how well they had turned out. He sent her the proofs from which she was to make a selection, certain that she would like them all.

A few days later her boyfriend came to the shop. "These are good pictures," he said, "but my girlfriend doesn't want them. She won't change her mind."

The photographer couldn't understand why this woman would not want a good picture of herself. Eventually he concluded that she must have resented the fact that a toy duck had broken through her reserve. Such a small thing, yet it may have seemed very demeaning to her. She allowed this vanity to come between herself and happiness.

A Lesson in Vanity

Vanity takes other forms, too. Several years ago an ECK initiate went through a period of doubt. "I've been studying ECK for ten years, and I'm only a Third Initiate. I'm tired of this. I want to move ahead." It bothered her quite a bit.

She went into contemplation and asked the Mahanta, "Why am I here? Why am I not farther along?"

On the inner planes she found herself in a meeting with four ECK Masters who were seated around a table. "You are very vain," they told her. "Because you have so much vanity, you are unable to surrender."

She came out of contemplation and thought about the answer she had received. But since she was overweight and very shy, she just could not accept vanity as the reason.

She tried again: "Mahanta, what's the real reason I'm here."

Soon after this, the ECK Masters Rebazar Tarzs and Peddar Zaskq (Paul Twitchell) came to her on the inner planes.

"Why are you in a fat body?" Rebazar asked her.

"So I won't take pride in my appearance," she answered.

"Why are you so shy?" Peddar Zaskq asked.

"I'm afraid of what people will think of my appearance," she said. Even at this point, she did not make the connection between her attitude and vanity.

"Ten years in ECK, and I'm still a Third Initiate," she complained to her husband. "I want God-Realization!" So she quit ECK and joined the Lutheran church. Keep in mind that this woman was very sincere. She was doing everything she could think of to reach the higher states of consciousness.

Many people do the same thing: They feel they are doing their best to go forward in ECK, but they run out of patience. If they could just be honest with themselves and accept the answers that the Master gives them, they would become aware of what stands between them and love; what they must do in order to surrender to the ECK. And then, if they would wait just another day, another week, things would turn around.

This woman attended church regularly and listened intently as the minister explained the Bible. But all the while her childhood guide, an ECK Master, was there with her, interpreting the truth within the scriptures in a way the minister only half understood.

"Thou shalt love the Lord thy God," the minister recited. "Thou shalt love thy neighbor as thyself." She now found new meaning in these familiar words. She began to realize that she could not love God or her neighbor until she first learned to love herself; and she couldn't do that until she surrendered the vanity within herself. The struggle went on.

She and her husband moved several times over the years. At one point she underwent an operation that caused her to lose a lot of weight. For the first time in years, she was able to move about more easily. Her self-confidence grew as she discovered that she was attractive to others again. But now that her outer life was so great, the inner experiences began to slow down.

When she had grown very comfortable with her life, trouble cropped up in her marriage. She and her husband had each asked the Master in their own way, "Show me what love is. Show me how to love someone." But when the answer came, it wasn't what they wanted.

When people ask for help or truth, the answer often comes in a way they did not expect. "No, that can't be right," they protest. So they continue on as before, now and then saying, "Oh, God, I've asked for guidance—why aren't you helping me?" This is what the woman did.

Eventually her husband said he wanted a divorce, and her comfortable life was shattered. At first she resisted, but over a period of time she thought it out more thoroughly. Finally she reached a decision: If I love my husband so much, the supreme act of love would be to let him go. She made up her mind to tell him later that day when they met for lunch.

That resolved, she went to take a shower. As she stood beneath the stream of water, she suddenly felt the golden Light of ECK come into her. It hadn't happened in years. She knew then that her act of love was her act of surrender. Though she was losing the human love, this surrender allowed her to receive the divine love.

She wrote to me and requested permission to study the ECK discourses once again. Along with her first discourse she was advised that, as a new student of ECK, she could expect her First Initiation within six to twelve months. Her heart almost broke as she realized how much she had lost. Before she had been a Third Initiate; now she wasn't even a First. Not only had her outer life been swept out from under her, but she had lost the ECK initiations of the past.

How can my outer initiations be taken away when my inner unfoldment is there? she wondered. She didn't recognize at the time, of course, that the inner unfoldment wasn't there.

In the meantime, she has come to understand that a lag between the inner and the outer had existed within her, and this is what caused so much of her struggle. Now she is back on the path of ECK and has regained the spiritual unfoldment that she lost before.

Learning Soul Travel

A problem for many initiates, even the Higher Initiates, is their inability to learn how to Soul Travel. The reason is that they try it for a little while, then give up too soon. Or they aren't very inventive or creative with the spiritual exercises, and go through them as routinely as if they were reciting the rosary. The result: no inner experiences, no dream travel, no Soul Travel, no nothing. Of course they wonder, Why doesn't it work?

The spiritual life takes more effort than doing the spiritual exercises by rote. It means putting yourself into it wholeheartedly.

A manuscript came across my desk by an individual who described his plodding, step-by-step efforts to learn

Soul Travel. I said, "Hey, that's exactly how I did it when I was trying to learn." It was a very good primer on how to do the spiritual exercises. I passed it on to the editors, who made the revisions needed to bring out the spiritual content.

The author was open and agreeable to the changes. He felt his experiences would be of value to other initiates. "Do whatever you want with the manuscript," he said. And this is how Terrill Willson's book, *How I Learned Soul Travel,* came to be published.

Arranged in short chapters, the book describes each step the author took as he tried one technique after another with varying degrees of success. After a couple of years, he went through a period where he wondered if he was a failure at it.

Each time a person reaches a higher plane of unfoldment, it seems as if the laws reverse: what worked before all of a sudden does not. As the author came through this entire series of learning how to move into the higher states of consciousness through Soul Travel, he was finally able to realize he hadn't failed at all, but was ready to go on to greater things.

Freedom Takes Effort

People who say, "Please take my bad dreams away," don't realize that if the dreams were taken away from them and the karma was released in their outer life, it would create hardships that are totally unnecessary in ECK. Instead, they can work it out by giving it to the Mahanta and letting it be resolved in the best possible way. The Mahanta, the Living ECK Master is here for just that purpose.

I spend just about every hour of every day working on

ways to make the message of ECK just a little clearer, to help people understand that truth is just at their fingertips. But some effort must be made for spiritual freedom. That is why justification by faith won't do it. Yet, one doesn't have to live under the sword of karma or retribution either. There is a way to soften life, to make it one filled with love, and this is what I am trying to show people.

Love Is Stronger than Death

An ECKist who worked as a counselor to students in various county schools awoke one morning feeling so tired and heavy that he couldn't get going. He thought about calling his supervisor to say he would be late, or, better yet, not go in at all. After a while, he dragged himself into the shower, forced down some breakfast, and started to get dressed, but all he really wanted to do was go back to bed. By this time he was very late for work.

While he was trying to make up his mind what to do, he suddenly realized that his fatigue was gone. He finished dressing, then got in his car and headed for work.

As he drove down the street, he noticed a boy sitting on a curb, crying. He wondered what was wrong. The Law of Noninterference seemed to suggest that he should just mind his own business and drive on by. On the other hand, he thought, the Law of Love supersedes all.

He pulled over to the curb and called out to the boy, "Do you want a ride?" Normally he would never encourage a child to accept a ride from a stranger, but this case felt like an exception.

The boy tentatively walked over to the car, tears streaming down his cheeks. The ECKist unlocked the door to let him in. "Let's go for a ride and talk," he said.

They drove along in silence for a while, to allow the boy a little time to compose himself. Finally the ECKist asked the boy, "Why are you crying?"

"I just got suspended from school," the boy said.

"Why?"

"The teacher told us to write a paper on a love relationship we have with someone. I wrote about my parents."

"Why would that cause a suspension?" the ECKist asked.

"My parents died in a car wreck four years ago," the boy explained. "But they come to me in dreams, and I know they're always with me. That's the only love relationship I have. That's why I wrote about it."

The ECKist was intrigued by this story. "What happened when you handed in your paper?" he asked.

"The teacher read it in front of the class and made fun of me. He said I hadn't adjusted to the death of my parents, and that I needed counseling."

Why would the teacher say such a thing to a boy in front of his classmates? The ECKist could imagine the effect that would have on a child.

The boy went on to say that he was sent to the principal's office, then taken to see the school counselor. Together they tried to convince him that the visits from his parents were not real, they were just figments of his imagination.

"That's not so," the boy protested. "I actually see them. It's just the way I wrote it."

"You're imagining the whole thing," they insisted.

"No, I'm not," he said. "It's true."

When he continually refused to admit that he had made up the story, they got fed up with him and sent him home on a three-day suspension. He had just left the school when the ECKist drove by and saw him sitting on the curb.

"I bet you don't believe me either," the boy said defensively.

"Oh, I wouldn't say that." The ECKist knew in certain instances people who had left the physical body were able to keep in contact with loved ones, for the bond of love is stronger than death.

"Have you ever heard of ECKANKAR?" the boy asked. The question just came out of the blue, and the ECKist was taken completely by surprise. Without a word, he took his left hand off the steering wheel and held it out to show the boy his ECK insignia ring. The boy took one look, and burst into tears all over again.

He began to tell the ECKist a little more about himself. He was ten years old and living on the West Coast when his parents, both ECK initiates, were killed in an automobile accident. Since there were no other relatives, he was made a ward of the state. Checking into his background, the California officials discovered that he was originally from the East Coast, so they sent him back to the state of his birth. He was placed in a foster home with a family of Seventh-Day Adventists, who constantly tried to convert him to their beliefs.

For four long years, this young boy had held fast to the ECK teachings he had studied with his parents, which his parents continued to impart to him in the dream state. But on this particular day, as he sat all alone on the curb, he wondered if the Mahanta had forgotten him.

"Would you like me to go back to school with you and try to straighten this out?" the ECKist offered. As a counselor for the county, he was acquainted with the principal of that school. The boy said yes, he would like that very much.

They went back to the school and had a meeting with the principal, who confirmed the boy's story.

"This isn't a matter of lying," the ECKist said. "It's a matter of freedom of religion. ECKANKAR is this boy's religion, and it teaches that Souls are able to communicate in the dream state with their loved ones if they so choose."

The principal looked doubtful.

"Furthermore," the ECKist added, "I am a member of ECKANKAR, too, and I share his beliefs."

The principal quickly backed down. "There has obviously been some misunderstanding here," he said. "We'll get him back in class immediately."

The boy held firmly to the teachings of ECK under conditions far more difficult than most adults have to endure. Completely defenseless except for his link to the Mahanta and the connection with his deceased parents, on that day it had seemed as if it was all being taken away from him. Where is the protection? he wondered. Where is the love? Through his contact with the ECKist, he found that the protection and the love were right here, and now he knows that life has much to offer him.

Count Your Blessings

A Higher Initiate wanted to be more open to love. He asked me if there was a special technique for greater surrender that would bring this about.

There is a technique, but unlike other spiritual exercises, it does not have a beginning, middle, and end. This technique involves attitude, and it is one that must be lived. In a word, it's called gratitude.

The power of gratitude opens the heart to allow love to enter. But once the love comes in and we receive the gifts of Spirit and of life, the way to keep the gifts flowing is through an ongoing spirit of gratitude. People are usually too busy counting the things they don't have. They notice how much more money their neighbor has, how much further ahead in spiritual unfoldment someone else is, and so on. But if we stop to count our blessings, to realize how much we do have and be grateful for it, then the heart is kept open to love and all the gifts that love brings.

I wish there were some easy technique I could give you to feel gratitude. There are times when it will seem difficult, but it's really as simple as appreciating what you have in your life.

If there is someone you love, let that person know how you feel. Say thank you to your mate or your child even when you don't feel well. If you can just stop and be grateful for the blessings that are before you, your heart will open to love. Then the blessings can keep coming.

May the blessings be.

ECKANKAR International Creative Arts Festival,
Chicago, Illinois, June 20, 1987

Until you learn something for yourself, it's like listening to a tape of a thunderstorm. Only the real thing can make the windows of Soul rattle.

13

Protection of the Master

Several of us were discussing how women worry about gaining weight and men worry about losing hair.

Viewpoints

One fellow mentioned that when he was younger, he used to laugh at how artful some of the older men got with the comb. They'd bring the hair up very nicely from the sides, all the way over to the center, then make a part down the middle. Others raised the art to an even higher state by bringing their hair up from the back and curving it over the top.

He now has only the greatest respect for those wise men and is glad he took the time to watch and study them. What he used to call combing he now thinks of as proper placement of hair.

These are some of the things we do which, though not essential to spiritual unfoldment, fill the space between here and there. We do what it takes to keep ourselves in the best condition we can, because the spiritual life encompasses the total being. This includes our physical, emotional, mental, and spiritual welfare.

If our physical condition is such that our body doesn't work as well as other people's, we can still appreciate our mental, emotional, and spiritual states. We try to find the positive elements in life by being grateful for the blessings that we do have.

The Real Thing

I used to enjoy listening to tapes of the sounds of nature while I worked. My favorite was the tape of a thunderstorm, which was especially refreshing during a long dry spell we had in Minnesota. Then spring came and brought the real thing. I was reminded of the difference between an artificial and a real thunderstorm. A real thunderstorm causes the windows to rattle. Ever since then, I just haven't been able to enjoy that tape.

It's a little bit like the time I described a certain spiritual experience, and a detractor of ECK responded with, "Well, a lot of people have experiences like that." From the outside looking in, from the viewpoint of one who has never experienced the real thing, I guess that's how he saw it.

No matter what you say or how long you talk, you will never convince someone who doesn't know anything about the Light and Sound of God. He may nod in agreement and understand exactly what you are saying with his head, but he will never know it in his heart. Knowing with the heart comes only through actual experience with some aspect of the ECK, the Holy Spirit, which comes as Sound or Light. This is what I try to bring about in the students of ECK.

I try my best to simplify the things I have learned for myself and pass them on to you. But until you learn it for yourself, it's like listening to a tape of a thunderstorm. Only the real thing can make the windows of Soul rattle.

Competition vs Gratitude

The funny thing is that when a person does have some kind of an experience, he tends to measure it against someone else's. He says, "I have Light all the time, but I would like to hear the Sound." Or, "I get the Sound but I would like to see the Master." Or, "I have Soul traveled but I haven't this or that."

There is nothing wrong with striving for more as long as we remember to be grateful for the blessings we do have. This is sometimes difficult. We are trained from childhood to strive for the things we do not have, and so we are always competing.

Competition means putting one's attention on what he doesn't have and therefore hopes to accomplish. Gratitude, on the other hand, is knowing that the gift is already given and one has only to open himself to receive it. Gratitude not only opens the heart to receive the gifts of the Holy Spirit but allows the gifts to keep on coming. This is why it is so important.

A Panhandler's Gift

An ECK initiate who worked as a waitress was approached in a parking lot by a young mother carrying a baby. "I don't have any money, and my baby is sick," she said. "Can you give me some money for groceries?" Though the ECKist didn't have much money herself, she gave the woman twenty dollars.

Thinking about it later, she wondered if the young mother really intended to use the money rightfully. What if she spends it on drugs or drink? the ECKist wondered. Maybe I've aided this woman in cementing a bad habit. By giving her the money, did I encourage her to continue panhandling? Did I do the right thing? Was this the right way to go about being an ECKist?

Then a realization came to her: Everything she had was of the ECK. If the ECK said to give, it was not for her to question. How it was used by the person who received it was not her responsibility. If she had it to give and gave it with a clear, loving heart, this is all that was important. So she stopped worrying about it.

The next night at work, for some reason the customers she served were more generous than usual with tips, and in a short time she made more than the money she had given away. Once again she realized that everything comes from the ECK—not only what we have in hand and can see at this moment, but much more that we cannot see. It's just waiting to be received with an open, grateful heart.

I'm not suggesting that you throw money at every panhandler who comes along. But there will be occasions when the ECK, the Mahanta, says to you: "This is a time to give." The giving may prove to be more of a gift for you than for the person who's getting. From giving come the realizations which uplift the consciousness. And this upliftment of the spiritual consciousness is what we are concerned with in ECK.

The Master doesn't take something away and leave a void; something better is always given back. Of course, there may be a few minutes or days or weeks when our hands appear to be empty. But it's only because it may take a little time for the greater gift to come and replace the possession or karma which was taken away.

Karma is removed to make way for something better—but will we receive the gift? Sometimes we resist. "I'm used to this," we say. "I want to hold on to it." The Master doesn't ever force the issue.

The Pretty-Book Syndrome

At five-and-a-half years of age, my daughter displayed a certain knack for dealing with younger children of about three. She seemed to know just how to work with them. One afternoon when I picked her up from her kindergarten class, I watched her walk up to a little girl and take away a book. The child relinquished it without a fuss. Later I said to my daughter, "I saw you take that book away from the little girl. How did you do it without making her cry?"

"I'll show you," she said. She handed me a book. "Now this is a very pretty book, isn't it?"

"It's a very pretty book," I agreed, playing along.

"Hang on real tight," she instructed. "You're not going to give it to me, OK?"

"No way."

She pulled and tugged at the book, but I hung on tightly. "See?" she said. "The kid won't let go."

She went over to the bookcase, took another book out, and brought it back to me. "See how much bigger this book is and how pretty the cover is." She flipped it open to show me the nice pictures. "Isn't this book pretty?" she said.

"Yes, it is."

"Here," she said, holding it out to me. As I reached out for it with one hand, she very nimbly snatched the first book from my other hand. "See how easy it is?" she said.

The first time I noticed her toddling around by my bookcase at age two and a half, I figured the only way to keep her from tearing out the pages was to teach her the value of books. She caught on quickly, and in time she came to think of them as precious objects. But even more precious than books were her teddy bears.

When she had finished her book-taking demonstration,

I grabbed up one of her teddy bears. "How are you gonna get *this* away from me, hmmm?"

This time she didn't bother with psychology. She marched right up to me, grasped the teddy bear's arm, and yanked it out of my hands. "That's how," she said. "Then you rush around the room and find something to give to the baby so he won't cry."

This is how I learned that there's one rule for precious and another rule for very precious.

A Boy and a Toy Tiger

Someone sent me a book of cartoons based on the comic strip *Calvin and Hobbes.* The artist has a very good insight into the spiritual nature of children and a wonderful ability to see things from a child's viewpoint. When we grow up, we actually forget what it was like to be a child. We forget that adults don't even exist in a child's world unless the child allows us in — and then only according to certain terms. He keeps the key to his little world in his pocket, and if he doesn't like us, he'll just go numb and lock us out.

In the cartoon strip Calvin is a little boy, and Hobbes is a tiger. When the boy's parents are around, Hobbes is just a stuffed animal with a flat nose. But as soon as they leave Calvin alone, Hobbes turns into a very smart, talkative tiger with a nice rounded nose.

In one story, Hobbes is left in the car while the little boy goes inside with his parents. Hobbes leans out the window and says to Calvin, "Ask your dad if he'll leave the car keys so I can listen to the radio."

Grownups and children really do live in two different worlds. To the child the stuffed tiger is alive and very real. Children are not lying when they talk about many of the experiences they have with their toy animals or invisible friends.

My daughter used to have so many stuffed animals in her room that she barely had enough space left to get into bed. "Some of these creatures will have to go," I said to her. We simply didn't have enough money to rent a larger place with an extra bedroom for the animals. As difficult as it was for her to let go of any of them, we went through her room and cleaned out the least favorites, leaving only the most loved ones. You can always tell the favorites by how dirty they are.

Releasing Old Habits

The protection of the Master works like that, too. We clutch to ourselves certain habits and patterns we think are so precious, without realizing that they are actually causing us problems. And like the child who took away a book to replace it with a better one, the Master tries to remove an old habit to replace it with something better. Our part is to recognize that it's better and accept the gift.

As people get older many of the old patterns, such as anger, hang on. Before one comes into ECK, the karma incurred by these old habits is paid off more slowly. Karma created in 1967 may not come back for twenty or thirty years or more. The two events—the cause and the effect—are spread so far apart that the individual never recognizes the connection. Therefore, because he doesn't know that the troubles of today are actually the paying off of karma he made for himself back in 1967, he goes right along doing the same things, always creating new karma.

One of the advantages of the spiritual path of ECK is that the cause and effect are brought very close together. The Master usually speeds up the karmic payment so we can make a connection between our act of anger and the ill fortune it is causing us.

Boiling Mad

An ECKist pulled up to the drive-through window at a fast-food restaurant and sat out there for ten minutes without getting waited on. He got so boiling mad that he left his wife in the car and stomped inside to give someone a piece of his mind.

He really let the manager have it. When he was finished, he went back out to the car and saw that steam was coming from under the hood. A radiator hose had broken causing the radiator to boil over.

"What is it?" his wife asked.

Instead of saying it was a broken radiator hose, he simply said, "A symbol." She knew what he meant.

It doesn't take much to figure out the connection when you're boiling mad and a minute later find your car radiator boiling over. In return for the ill will you imposed on another, you now have the inconvenience of repairing the car. Because the cause and effect are close together, you realize the spiritual lesson.

The Shortcut

An ECKist bought a telephone from a store in an unfamiliar part of town. When the phone wouldn't operate the way it was supposed to, he decided to take it back to the store and raise a fuss. Partway there, he saw a road he thought would be a shortcut. But the road swerved off in a different direction than he expected, and he soon realized he was lost.

While he was trying to find his way out of the maze of unfamiliar streets, he glanced at the gas gauge. He was almost out of fuel. Not only could he not find the store, but he hadn't brought enough money with him to buy gas, and it looked like he would run out any minute. Now he was really furious.

He drove a little further, lost in his angry thoughts, when all at once the point of what was happening trickled through: Running out of fuel meant he was running out of ECK. The ECK wasn't with him while he was so angry. When he took a minute to put the whole situation in perspective, he was able to laugh at himself for blowing it so out of proportion.

He dug through his pockets and found enough change to buy the gas he needed to get home. On the way, he saw a street that led to the store where he had bought the phone. The clerk took care of the problem, and he got home without further incident.

It was impatience that impelled him to try the shortcut. Impatience is just a child of anger.

Some people spend so much time looking for ways to cheat the game. There are no shortcuts in the spiritual life. We like to think there is an easy way to beat our karma, that we can do whatever we want and somehow, maybe by the old belief in justification by faith, get past the problem with no payback. But it really doesn't work that way.

Protected from Serious Injury

An ECK initiate in British Columbia had just gotten a car. One winter afternoon she traveled to a town many miles from home. Her husband met her there in his own car.

After a couple of hours, she decided to go home and get started on some chores. Her husband wanted to stay a little longer, so he said he would be home later.

She inched her way carefully along roads made treacherous by the newly fallen snow. Ever so cautiously she eased the car around a sharp curve. But as she came out of the turn, she hit an icy spot and found that she had no control over the car whatsoever.

Very calmly she began to chant HU. In what seemed like slow motion, the car slid off the road, tumbled down a steep bank, and rolled over, loose objects flying out through the shattered windows. The car finally landed on its wheels facing the direction from which she had come.

She unhooked her seat belt and stumbled out of the car. A woman who witnessed the accident yelled down from the road that she would call the Royal Canadian Mounted Police and an ambulance. Sore all over, the ECKist couldn't even attempt to climb back up to the road. Other people came along with blankets to wrap her in. Soon the ambulance arrived.

With siren screaming and lights flashing, the ambulance rushed through the night to a hospital in the town she had just been visiting. Fortunately, she had no serious injuries. Treated and released, she called a friend who lived in town to come and pick her up. They went back to the friend's house and just sat around sipping tea and talking.

The phone rang, and it was her husband calling to find out if she was there. He had just gotten home and was relieved that she had decided to stay in town and visit with her friend. "I just heard on the news that there was a terrible accident," he said. "I'm just glad you're not on the road." The car shown on the news didn't resemble the one he had seen his wife driving that afternoon.

She didn't quite know how to break it to him. Finally she told him what had happened and assured him she was fine. She had been listening to an ECK tape as she drove and had chanted HU when the car went out of control. Knowing how much worse it could have been, she recognized that the hand of the Master had protected her from serious injury.

The Invisible Forest

A woman who lived in Oregon had been dreadfully afraid of snow all her life. She didn't mind it as long as it was just laying there, but when it was falling or blowing, she became terribly afraid.

Through her experiences on the inner planes, she was made aware of the contributing causes of her attitude. She understood that a karmic situation from a past life had shown up in this life as unreasonable fear of blowing or falling snow.

When she received a job offer from a firm in Colorado, she decided to go there for an interview. Her husband was willing to relocate if she thought the position worthwhile, but he was unable to make the trip with her. That meant a long drive by herself through Oregon, Idaho, Wyoming, then to Colorado.

About a week before she was to leave, a winter storm blanketed the area with snow. All week long she thought about canceling the interview, but the Inner Master kept saying: "Take the trip as planned. Everything's OK."

She left home early in the morning and traveled throughout the first day without incident. Late in the afternoon of the second day, she arrived in a town in Wyoming that seemed a good place to stop for the night. She wondered if she should push on to the next town, even though the towns in that area of Wyoming are spread so far apart that it would be quite a long drive. She wasn't sure what to do.

"Everything is OK," the Inner Master said. "Keep going."

She continued on to the next town.

On the way she ran into a snowstorm. Visibility was so bad that she couldn't even see the road ahead. Terrified, she began to chant HU. The snowfall soon dwindled to a stop.

All of a sudden she realized she was driving through a forest, which effectively blocked the snow on both sides of the road. The tall trees showed clearly in the headlights, and she noticed that the roadsides were dotted with picnic tables and scenic little trails. Someday I'm going to come back and explore these paths, she thought.

The forest ended just before she reached her destination, and up ahead she saw the bright lights of the city. She was so thankful that she had taken that road through the forest.

The interview went well, and she accepted the job. A few weeks later she and her husband loaded up a rental truck with their belongings and began the drive to Colorado. On the second day of their trip, another snowstorm hit. "Don't worry," she told her husband. "Pretty soon this road will go through a forest, and the driving is easy there."

Several miles later they still hadn't come to the forest. The snow was falling even heavier than before. "It can't be much farther," she said.

Hour after hour they drove; still no forest. She couldn't figure out why. At last they saw the lights of the city. All at once she understood what had happened: The sudden appearance of the forest at a time when she had been so frightened was the special protection of the Master.

The initiate had been raised in consciousness to a level where the forest existed. It was in a higher area of the physical plane which exists at a rate of vibration just beyond the normal physical senses. The forest hadn't been visible when she passed by with her husband simply because the need wasn't there.

The laws of nature can be bent when there is a need for protection or for a spiritual lesson. Usually the experience is given as a way for an individual to learn something that could not be learned any other way. He is raised to a higher state of consciousness much in the same way as when he travels to a Temple of Golden Wisdom.

The Great-aunt

A teenage ECKist went to her great-aunt's home for dinner one night. After dinner, the adults sat in the dining room talking, and the teenager went into the living room to watch TV. One of the great-aunt's friends was a fire-breathing evangelist who had very little regard for other people's right to believe as they wished—especially ECKists. She followed the girl into the living room and started to read her the riot act on religion, which amounted to threats of hell and damnation.

Teenagers have a wonderful ability to tune out what they don't want to hear. As far as they're concerned, you're not even there. You can holler to your heart's content; all they'll do is look straight ahead with a blank stare. They don't even blink. It's like being in the presence of a stone statue.

Later the girl mentioned to her mother that this woman had really laid a trip on her about hellfire and brimstone. "I know that none of it is true," she said. "It was a nuisance, but I was nice about it and just let her talk." The ECK child was being far more gracious than the woman had been.

The girl's mother brought the matter to the attention of the great-aunt. But though she was not of the same denomination as her evangelistic friend, the aunt shared her belief that a Christian's mission in life was to see that everybody else was saved. Therefore, she saw no reason to defend her grandniece against this intrusion. The subject became a real sore spot in that family.

The great-aunt mentioned that she was planning a trip to Israel, but a couple of her friends had said they'd had some bad dreams about it. "Don't go," they warned her. "It would be a dangerous trip for you to take."

"I'm going anyway," she said. "If the Lord doesn't want me to go, he'll let me break my ankle or something."

Two days later the great-aunt went out to the garage, missed a step, and fell and broke her collarbone. Naturally she didn't connect the incident to the Master's protection of the ECK initiate. Maybe she thought it was the Lord's way of stopping her from the dangers awaiting her in Israel.

Soon after that, the great-aunt again allowed the evangelist to unleash her religious beliefs on her visiting grandniece. Within two weeks, the great-aunt tripped and broke her ankle.

Her evangelist friend came over to see how she was doing and began to preach a long, rambling sermon on sin and damnation. Totally helpless, her collarbone and ankle broken, the great-aunt had no choice but to stay seated in the rocking chair and listen to this woman. For the first time, she got the full impact of what the teenager had been subjected to.

"That was the worst sermon I've ever heard," she said later. "I'll never let her preach like that to my grandniece again!" Now that it had happened to her, she was able to make the connection: The evangelist had violated the

ECKist's space. Since it had taken place in her home, the great-aunt, as the girl's hostess, should have protected her from this invasion. Even though the aunt wasn't an ECKist, within a very short time she had gotten all the lessons of an ECKist, one piled on top of the other.

Search for Katsupari

The Katsupari Monastery is one of the Temples of Golden Wisdom on the physical plane. Two ECK initiates who work closely with the ECK Office came across some old books that made reference to a Katsupari Monastery in the Indian state of Sikkim. Could this be the Katsupari that Paul Twitchell had spoken of? they wondered.

It wasn't, really, but it was something they had to pursue for their own spiritual learning. Like the quest for the Holy Grail, the important thing is not finding the grail, but what you've learned in your search for it. They had to go there first, to find out for themselves that this was not the Katsupari Monastery of the ECK writings. Paul always gave the location as northern Tibet, some five or six hundred miles north of the one in Sikkim. This one probably took its name from the original, the way Paris, Kentucky, took its name from Paris, France. There really is no comparison between the two.

These two initiates went through a great deal of personal danger in their quest. Revolutions were going on in the area, and entry by westerners was greatly restricted. But the trip was necessary for them, and so the ECK opened the way.

It was very slow going. They had to hike uphill through a junglelike area along a leech-infested trail. They carried salt with them to sprinkle over their shoes in an attempt to keep the things from slithering over their feet and legs.

But they figured if the monks had it in mind to protect the monastery from the insincere, what better way than building it at the top of a steep ridge with the only access being a trail infested with leeches?

What they found on the hill in Sikkim was not the Katsupari ECK Wisdom Temple, but a two-room monastery in partial ruin. Surveying the grounds, they finally recognized the reason for their strong call to make this journey. In a past life they had been monks here and had often walked up the leech-strewn trail.

The original Katsupari Monastery that Paul spoke of is a castlelike structure with about seventy-five rooms and fifty monks, three of whom guard the Shariyat-Ki-Sugmad. It is a place one visits in the dream state, in the Soul body, to study under the ECK Masters. Some may get there in the physical body, but it's doubtful.

It is important for us to check things out for ourselves. A trip like this was not for what the two initiates found at the end of the rainbow, but what they found on the road to the end of the rainbow. It changed both of these individuals, and for them it was worth the effort.

The Katsupari Monastery is in the Mountain world. There is another Temple of Golden Wisdom in the Desert world and yet another in the Earth world. These are not on the Astral Plane; they are on the Physical Plane but at higher levels of consciousness where people with purely physical vision would likely not see them. Certain people who travel there can see them, but very few will.

Spiritual Tests

In *Soul Travelers of the Far Country* I describe some of the experiences I had on the inner planes with Peddar Zaskq, Rebazar Tarzs, and others. But more importantly,

I try to convey the hand-in-glove connection between the inner and the outer planes — what was involved, the spiritual tests I was required to undergo, the heartbreak, and how all the events led up to October 22, 1981.

I understand what people are going through when they say they are having very difficult times. Sometimes I cry with them. As you get into the higher states of consciousness on your way to becoming an ECK Master, you are going to have to go through it all. A lot of you take it quite patiently.

The carrot is held out in front of you, making you feel you are a grand one, and then it's snatched away. It's held out again, and just as you get your hopes up, once again it's snatched away. Pretty soon you don't even care if there is a carrot out there or not; you know you are here simply to live, move, and have your being in the ECK, as a clear channel for It.

Writing for ECK

I received a letter from an initiate who works with computers. He also wants to do some writing. Working with computers is a joy, he said, while trying to write is agony. He hopes he can somehow get the joy into his writing as well.

Writing for ECK is pretty much a combination of agony and ecstasy. You're happy when it comes out in a way you feel the ECK wants it brought out; yet you realize that human language is so inadequate to express the things that need to be said. I know there must be a better, fresher way to express what the ECK is trying to bring through. When it doesn't come, it's agony; and when it does come out correctly, which is seldom, it's ecstasy.

I find writing difficult, and so I take a great amount

of time with it. I always keep in mind that it's for you, that there has to be something in it for you. The whole intent is to make it relevant enough for you to understand.

I know that many of you are running into hardships in your travels, but at the same time you also run into realizations that the ECK is giving you. This is what we are here for.

My love goes with you always.

ECKANKAR International Creative Arts Festival, Chicago, Illinois, Sunday, June 21, 1987

"If you can learn that there are times when you have to stoop, you'll get through life very nicely," the minister told Ben Franklin. "But if you feel you must always stand straight, you're going to bump your head."

14

What Is the HU?

The title of this evening's talk is "What Is the HU?" By the time the talk is over, I think you will understand more about the power of HU and its place in refreshing Soul and lifting you spiritually.

Our closest association with HU often is during our spiritual exercises. The rest of our time is spent trying to see the spiritual lessons in our daily life.

Part of my job is to find the stories and different viewpoints that can be used to illustrate how the ECK actually works in our lives. I am constantly looking for ways to keep the message of ECK fresh for you, but so often I find that the message is very much the same—the same truth wearing different clothing.

Life in ECK

A Higher Initiate mentioned that she had worked backstage at the ECK European seminars for a number of years. But this year, she said, the ECK told her that she should be working at the front of the stage. There were many people that she needed to talk with, both for her own unfoldment and for their understanding.

Those of you who have been in ECK for any length of time realize that the only way to unfold is by giving to life. You give of yourself, not necessarily in the way that you feel is important, but in a way the ECK would have you pass Its love along to those who need it. Sometimes it's just a matter of listening to someone who needs to talk.

The ECK works in our lives whether we realize it or not. Even though we may not be conscious of it, the ECK brings to us, through the Mahanta, the spiritual experiences we need.

Some of the letters that cross my desk are truly heartrending. I know the people who are asking for help will be given the help. But it may not always come as quickly as they feel they need it or as quickly as I would like for them to have it.

Sometimes I would like to snap my fingers and say, "Worry no more--you are healed." But the ECK, in Its divine intelligence, may deem that this kind of an instant healing would be a disservice to one who is truly working to return home to God. Instant cures are often temporary healings which do very little to teach the individual the reason for his illness, sadness, or heartbreak.

The teachings of ECK work on the simple principle that love is the divine current which makes all life possible. We as Soul ride on this current, first of all, away from God. Then, at the farthest point away, at the very end of Its rope, Soul finds the teachings of ECK and can return home.

End of Illusion

Before this, Soul has despaired of ever finding truth, of ever finding the best way home to God. Throughout Its many sojourns, in Its many lifetimes on earth and on the inner planes, Soul has been granted boons such as instant healings and "undeserved" riches. All too often the individual has been misled to believe that life is a free ride or that life gives its bounties only to the fortunate. This misunderstanding has brought confusion.

But when we come to ECK, we find that the games of illusion come to an end. We stop believing in all the lies that say we can get something for nothing. Finally we reach the understanding that everything we do, everything that happens to us, is for our own spiritual good and of our own making. At the end of the road we realize that the spiritual path is about love for all, self-responsibility, and responsibility to all life.

Learning to Stoop

Benjamin Franklin was one of the most admired men in the world. To this day he remains a prominent figure in the American gallery of heroes. Among his many accomplishments, he helped draft the Declaration of Independence and was one of the signers of the Constitution of the United States.

Franklin believed strongly in making use of the lessons of experience. One such valuable lesson about life was learned through a small misfortune that took place when he was a young man.

Arriving at minister Cotton Mather's home for a visit, he entered by the front door and was shown to the study. There the two men talked for some time. At the end of the visit, still in conversation, they left the study. Franklin walked slightly ahead of the minister, looking back over his shoulder as they talked. The minister motioned Franklin down a narrow, dimly-lit hallway that led to an exit out of the side of the house. Having entered through the front,

Franklin had no way of knowing the hazards of this corridor.

Walking almost backward now, Franklin made another comment.

"Stoop! Stoop!" the minister said.

Franklin was trying to figure out what the man was talking about, when suddenly the back of his head collided with a low ceiling beam. Then he understood.

Cotton Mather took the occasion to point out an important lesson to the young Ben Franklin. "If you can learn that there are times when you have to stoop, you'll get through life very nicely," he said. "But if you feel you must always stand straight, you're going to bump your head."

Franklin learned the lesson, but he never took it far enough to tie it in with Soul's journey back home to God. He wasn't ready in that lifetime to realize that the spiritual lessons always form a complete circle, that any action always returns to the individual.

If one learns to exercise wisdom as he walks through life, he will know there are times he must bend—even as the tree in winter must bend under the weight of the snow—or break.

Two Kinds of Co-workers

There's an important distinction between being a Co-worker with the Mahanta and a Co-worker with the SUGMAD. A Co-worker with the Mahanta is one who is in training for ECK Mastership. When you give of yourself to bring the message of ECK to others, you are acting as a Co-worker with the Mahanta.

As you become perfected as a Co-worker with the Mahanta, you rise in states of consciousness to one day become a Co-worker with SUGMAD, or God. A Co-worker with God is one who has reached the state of God-Realization and fully understands his spiritual relationship with the SUGMAD.

The Mahanta is the highest state of consciousness on earth. The closest comparison that someone with a Christian background might make would be the Christ Consciousness.

Finding the Right Religion

Following the state of consciousness of your belief is important only if it leads to your spiritual betterment. If it does, then it is the right religion for you. If it doesn't, perhaps you owe it to yourself to find a religious teaching or way of life that will take you into a greater spiritual state of consciousness.

The final destination for Soul is not to become a perfected being in the absolute sense. In ECK we know that the process of perfection goes on and on. You become the best that you can be in your life today, thereby laying the groundwork for tomorrow. This is what the path of ECK shows you.

This is not something that can be accomplished through mental exercises or exertion of willpower. It comes through the discipline of divine love. By opening our heart to Divine Spirit, which is the ECK, we allow ourself to become an instrument for It and Its ways.

If we want to keep the blessings of life coming to us, we must learn to be grateful for what we have and for whatever is given. This gratitude begins to create a series of events for our spiritual benefit. It also allows us to get through the hardships we are enduring today because of something we did in the past. The gratitude is not for the hardship or the pain, of course, but for the lesson that Soul is reaping for Its own perfection so that It can one day become a Co-worker with God.

Consultation Time

The ECK often works through indirect measures. An initiate from California went to an ECKANKAR Creative Arts Festival hoping to have a consultation with me. But my schedule was so full that I simply couldn't see him. He was very disappointed.

After the seminar he went to the airport for the trip back home. At the boarding gate he ran into an Eighth Initiate who was taking the same flight, and they arranged to sit together.

The ECK knew of the initiate's need to discuss many spiritual questions that were on his mind, and therefore the fifteen-minute consultation with me didn't come about. Instead, the Mahanta sent the High Initiate to him. The circumstances of their meeting allowed him a greater amount of time to talk over the things he needed to know for his spiritual unfoldment.

Turning a Spiritual Corner

A man arrived at the airport for a flight from St. Louis to his home in California and was told that the travel agent who had made his reservations had neglected to get him a seat assignment. "We'll put you on the standby list," the St. Louis ticket agent said, "but you'll have to wait until all the other passengers have been seated." To add insult to injury, the agent wasn't able to guarantee him a seat in the nonsmoking section, as he had originally requested.

He was so upset that he began to mentally formulate a stiff letter of complaint to the president of the airline.

Not only did he have to wait for a seat that was supposed to be confirmed, but he, a nonsmoker, was forced to sit in the smoking section. He threw in a few other things he was sure would go wrong before the trip ended.

In the middle of his angry mental letter, he suddenly caught himself. Wait a minute, he thought. The Mahanta spoke about the Law of Gratitude at a recent ECK seminar. Maybe I'll feel better if I stop and examine what I have to be grateful for.

Once he got started, he found it wasn't very difficult at all. First of all, he was grateful that he had been able to buy a round-trip ticket at a discounted fare. He was even more thankful that he had a job that allowed him to afford the trip at all. And standby or not, at least he was assured of a seat on the plane out of St. Louis.

Just then the ticket agent called his name and gave him a sticker with his seat assignment. It was for a seat in first class. Now he had even more to be grateful for.

It's easy enough to assume the results would have been the same even if he had stayed in the anger band. The person with a logical mind or a lower state of consciousness would simply say, "I deserved that seat." He would never even consider an alternate possibility: that the blessing came from a change of attitude.

Because the initiate had changed his attitude, even in the face of disappointment and delays, he was able to see that there were many good things in his life. The lesson was learned; he now understood the Law of Gratitude. Therefore, it wasn't necessary for him to endure sitting with the smokers and being totally miserable on his journey back to California. Nor did he have to put himself through the further aggravation of writing a letter of criticism to the airline. The initiate had turned a corner in his spiritual understanding.

Often we too get right to the end of our rope. At this point we have a choice: lash out in anger, or count our blessings. Be angry or grateful. In ECK we come to realize that the darts of anger we shoot at situations and people come back to us very quickly, bringing only more pain and more trouble. So if only for self-preservation, we find it is best to let the situation rest, count our blessings, and plan more carefully the next time.

In this case, it was actually the initiate's responsibility to double-check with the travel agent and make sure his seating had been assigned all the way through. When he took it for granted, the lesson came back to him. It could have then gone even more wrong, but because he changed his attitude, it turned out all right.

Steps to Higher Consciousness

As we go farther in ECK, we make steps from the human state of awareness to the higher levels of consciousness through dreams, Soul Travel, and experiences with the Light and Sound. For those of you who are new to the teachings of ECK, I am putting more attention on the first step, the dream state. This will help you learn the validity of the inner planes in which you, as Soul, live, move, and have your being. The purpose is to lead you to a fuller awareness of yourself as a being who operates and meets people on all planes of existence. You then learn to work more fully as a Co-worker with the Mahanta, so that you too can earn your mastership.

As you work and travel on the inner planes, whether in the dream state or through Soul Travel, you are opening yourself for experiences in the Light and Sound of ECK, the Holy Spirit. These two elements of ECK are the purifiers of Soul. They uplift you into the higher states of being, where you begin to act and think in ways which will eventually create a better life for you. What we do in the present makes our future.

Hearing Crickets

A Higher Initiate in ECK, a nurse, wrote to me about her elderly parents. Her dad has Alzheimer's disease and had to be admitted to a convalescent home. Her mother, whom she describes as a very spiritual being, used to attend church but stopped going after her husband became ill. Her religion didn't have the answers to her spiritual questions.

One morning the mother woke up and called her daughter right away. "I think I'd better get a medical checkup," she said.

"Why?" her daughter asked.

"Something is wrong. I keep seeing flashing lights and hearing strange noises."

"What kind of sounds do you hear?" the daughter asked.

"Crickets," the mother answered. "I keep hearing crickets." She was very concerned that she might be developing a condition similar to her husband's.

The daughter recognized this as an experience with the Light and Sound of ECK. She took this opportunity to tell her mother more about ECK, explaining that these are some of the different ways in which the Holy Spirit speaks to Soul.

The ECK manifests through various sounds or colors of light which are perceived differently on each plane of consciousness. At the level of consciousness where her mother happened to be as she drifted into the dream state, the ECK manifested as the sound of crickets. At other times It can be heard as a flute, as falling rain, sparrows or other chirping birds, a choir—many different ways. These are uplifting, spiritual sounds which represent the ECK transforming Itself to correspond to the vibrations of the particular plane upon which It is heard.

From the ECK books we know that the flute generally means the Fifth, or Soul, Plane, but not always. Sometimes we hear a flute being played at an ECK seminar. But this is not to say we have to discount an experience just because it occurs in the physical. In its own way, the sound of the flute has struck a corresponding note on the Soul Plane.

Attributes of God-Realization

As you read the ECK books, you can find out where the different sounds or forms of light occur. Points like these are interesting to know as we travel the path home to God. But I think it's more important to recognize that the inner Sound, no matter which form It takes as you hear It, is the Holy Spirit.

It is coming in to uplift and make changes in you that will leave you different than you were yesterday. These changes begin at the Soul level, at the heart of you. Gradually they work their way out to your outer world, and in time your behavior begins to change. You become more ethical, your actions become higher.

But ethics and higher actions are not the goal of spiritual unfoldment any more than wisdom, power, and freedom are the goals of the seeker of God. Rather, they are attributes that come to one who has reached God-Realization. As the biblical saying goes, "Seek ye first the kingdom of God . . . and all these things shall be added unto you." It means simply that if you seek the highest, the rest of life will fall into place. And this is the role of HU.

The Dream Teachings

There are many ways the ECK works in the life of one who gives himself over to the principle of HU, the principle of God. One example concerns an individual who quit college several years ago to take a job. About a year later the Mahanta told him in the dream state, "Go back to college, and take a political-science course."

The man had absolutely no interest in political science. On the other hand, the Mahanta had spoken. He figured the education certainly couldn't do him any harm.

He enrolled in the course at a local university and applied himself to his studies. Eventually he met a group of poets on campus and started to spend time with them. Being an amateur poet himself, he found these people more to his liking than political-science majors.

The ECKist let a few of his new friends read some of his poetry and was very gratified when they said they liked it. "There's going to be an annual poetry conference at the state university," they told him. "Why don't you come?"

He accepted the invitation and arranged to give a reading of some of his poetry. There were important people in the audience who were highly enthusiastic about it. The result: a full scholarship to the state university which would end in a master's degree.

He found this especially interesting since he hadn't even earned his bachelor's degree. But the university was willing to give him enough credits for work experience that he only had to devote two more semesters to his bachelor's degree, then he could start working toward his master's.

The only hitch was his job. He didn't think his employers would be very understanding when his classes conflicted with work. Company policy was pretty clear on this point.

"We'll make an exception in your case," his boss assured him. "We'll rearrange your work hours so that you can attend your classes."

A year later, the initiate thought about what would have happened if he had ignored the dream experience. When the Mahanta, the Inner Master, told him it was time to take the political-science course, he could have said, "I'm a poet, not a political scientist." He would be doing the same thing today that he had been doing for many years. Nothing would have changed. But because he was in ECK, because he had learned how to go to the inner worlds in the dream state and trust the Inner Master, his life was completely different.

The Mahanta had seen a whole new avenue of experience that could be opened up for the initiate's spiritual unfoldment and overall good. But it was still up to the individual to take the Mahanta's instructions seriously. The Master opened the door, but it was the initiate who had to walk through it. That he did, making the best use of his study abilities and instincts to carry out what the Master had set in motion for him. This is an example of someone who has learned how to work with the dream teachings in ECK.

The ECK Dream 1 Discourses can help many of you learn to make the bridge from your present daily consciousness to the inner teachings, to the area where the highest truths can be gleaned. Here you can receive the information and knowledge to begin restructuring your life in ways that will be beneficial for you and others. This is meant quite literally, because the path of ECK recognizes that as one person unfolds, everyone is uplifted.

One of the intermediate steps between the time one

begins to study ECK and the time he becomes a full Co-worker with God is to reach the initiation of the Fifth Circle. It takes a number of years and many tests to become a Higher Initiate in ECK; yet only at this point does the journey back home to God begin in earnest.

Playing Cards

One afternoon a business owner was walking through his company warehouse. Behind a closed door he heard the unmistakable sound of playing cards being slapped down on a table. He immediately sought out the supervisor of the department. "It sounds like some of the people in your department are playing cards on company time," he said. "Please handle this and bring them to my office."

No company can run well unless everyone does his share, he thought. He wasn't going to let the culprits get away with this. Expecting three or four workers to be brought to him, he went back to his office to wait.

A few minutes later the supervisor came in, but he had only one man in tow. "This is the guy who was playing cards," he said. The boss looked up and was dismayed. The man standing before him was his own brother, who was helping out with special projects on a volunteer basis.

"What do you want me to do with him?" the supervisor said gruffly. Of course, had he known it was the boss's brother, his tone would have been more courteous.

"Well, uh, first of all, he's working here as a volunteer," the boss said. "And, well, he's my brother."

Seeing his boss's discomfort, the supervisor just nodded and quickly backed out of the office.

The business owner knew it would be bad for morale if word got around that his brother, even though a volunteer, was playing cards while the others worked. But naturally his approach was different than it would be with an employee.

"Were you on break?" he asked him.

"Yes," his brother said. "I worked through the lunch hour to finish the project you gave me, then I took a short break. I was playing solitaire when the supervisor came in and said you wanted to see me."

"Oh, I see," the boss said. He couldn't think of anything else to say about it, so he changed the subject. "How about going on to a second and third project?" he asked, and told him what they were.

"Actually, we should do the third project next," his brother said. He went on to explain why it was needed first.

"You're right," the boss agreed. "That's what we'll do."

He suddenly realized what was happening here. Before the supervisor brought the cardplayer in, the business owner had been prepared to play the master-to-servant role. But once he saw that it was his brother, his attitude changed. He recognized that he was speaking with him as an equal.

This is how it is with the initiates of the Fifth Circle, known in ECK as the Brothers of the Leaf. One may be the RESA (Regional ECK Spiritual Aide) for a certain area, who is on par with the boss of a company, but the projects that need to be done are achieved through teamwork by his or her Brothers of the Leaf.

Tests of Initiation

In ECK the new student is given many tests to see if he is worthy of the First Initiation, the Second, and so on. When the individual finally reaches the Fifth Plane, his relationship with himself on the spiritual path changes. No longer so much the student, he recognizes that he is

256

now learning under the direct guidance of the Mahanta.

The Master takes each initiate to the highest plane of God he is ready for at any given time; but the freedom and right of mobility that one earns by reaching the Fifth Plane would never be understood or appreciated by an initiate of the First Circle.

The First Initiation is given completely on the inner planes in the dream state. It generally happens anywhere from six to twelve months after one begins his studies in ECK. Some people recognize it and some do not. That doesn't matter. The important thing is that an inner experience does occur which very definitely marks the initial linkup of Soul with the ECK, the Light and Sound of God.

As a person goes farther along, the tests increase. But they aren't the kind that require you to take the semester over if you flunk. In the higher awareness of Soul, you know that something you chose to do this way could have been done that way, so some part of the experience can be salvaged. Therefore, you'll only have to take a certain part of the test over, and then you can go on to the next one.

The tests of Spirit are unlimited. They reach you through your personal experiences in a totally unique way that could not be appreciated by anyone else. Most people are not even aware of what is occurring. Yet, by the time you first realize that it might have been a test, you've covered considerable ground; you've become more aware. Eventually you get to the point where you recognize practically every test that is given to you.

The Power of Chanting

Someone told me a story—I don't know its source— that illustrates the power of chanting.

Some time ago there was a Benedictine monastery in France, an austere establishment where the ninety monks devoted their waking lives to a rigid schedule of work, liturgical prayer, and six to eight hours a day of chanting. This left no more than about four hours a night for sleep.

One day a new abbot was appointed to the monastery. His first task was to institute the reforms of the Second Vatican Council. He started by trying to eliminate the Latin liturgy and adopt the French, thereby using the tongue of the common people that everyone could understand. Some of the monks willingly went along with the change, others wished to continue with the old way of doing things, and still others wanted to use a mixture of both.

In a very short time the abbot managed to make the change completely over to the French liturgy.

He next made a study of the chanting habits of the monks, concluding that the six to eight hours a day could be better spent on something else. What the abbot didn't realize was that the monks were using the Gregorian and other chants to recharge themselves spiritually. This is what enabled them to work such a full daily schedule. Whereas most of us would consider it a hardship of the greatest degree, they were able to get along very nicely on only four hours of sleep.

Again the abbot had his way. But very soon after the monks stopped their chanting, there was a new development: They began to suffer from extreme fatigue. It got so bad that they could barely make it through their daily work schedule.

The monks held a meeting to talk over the problem. They finally decided that their tiredness came from getting only four hours of sleep. Discussing it with the abbot, they got his consent to get more sleep.

But even with the extra rest, the monks were unable

to shake their fatigue. Medical specialists were called in. They suggested several changes in the daily routine that would give the monks more energy, but nothing worked.

One of the doctors finally recommended a dietitian. After analyzing their eating habits, the dietitian determined that the cause of the monks' problem was their sparse diet. "All you eat are the vegetables that you grow and a little bit of fish. You're starving yourselves to death. You need a more balanced diet."

So the monks began to eat meat and potatoes. But now, on top of being even more fatigued, one by one they started to get sick. In just a matter of a few months, seventy monks were laid out flat in their cells, unable to perform their duties.

Then the abbot heard about a man who worked with sound as a healing aid. The man claimed that his experiments with a certain type of sound machine had proven beneficial. In desperation the abbot sent for him and filled him in on everything that had taken place in the months he had spent at the monastery.

"Have the monks resume chanting six to eight hours a day," the man said. "The sound of the chanting will heal them and give them back the strength to work."

Once again the monks began to chant several hours a day. They even went back to eating the semi-vegetarian diet that their order had followed for centuries. Within half a year, most of the monks were back to work. Healthy and strong, they were again able to maintain the traditional Benedictine schedule of work, prayer, and chanting, with only four hours of sleep a night.

This story gives a good example of the power of sound. But although the chants used by the monks were very good, most of us wouldn't want to spend six to eight hours a day at it.

What Is HU?

In ECK there is a higher chant that gets the same job done in just twenty minutes a day. It is known as the HU. Chanting HU or your secret word enhances your life and gives you strength. This is why I urge you so often to keep up your spiritual exercises.

HU is a holy name for God which will lift you into the higher worlds. But the name itself has even more meaning behind it. I would like to recommend a spiritual exercise which will be very beneficial to you in finding it out for yourself.

As you chant each long, drawn-out HU outwardly, keep asking inwardly, "What is HU?" Repeat the question mentally as many times as is comfortable for you, maybe two or three. In other words, with each outward HU, you are asking within, "What is HU? What is HU? What is HU?"

Baraka Bashad. May the blessings be.

ECKANKAR European Seminar, The Hague, The Netherlands, Saturday, July 18, 1987

He met people so preoccupied with their appearance
that they spent a fortune to dress up like peacocks, always
trying to be something they were not. They gave far too
much for the whistle.

15

Don't Give Too Much for the Whistle

The popular comic strip *Calvin and Hobbes* illustrates how the world of children is far different than the one their parents can see.

A Child's World

Calvin is a little boy who lives in his own world. When Calvin's parents are around, Hobbes is just a stuffed tiger with a flat nose and lifeless eyes. But as soon as the boy is alone with him, Hobbes comes alive: His features fill out, his eyes sparkle, he spouts all kinds of wisdom, and he is a good friend to the boy.

An initiate told me how she discovered that her four-year-old son had his own special world.

At bedtime one night, he said he was afraid to go to his room alone.

"Well, take your bear with you," she suggested.

"I can't sleep with the bear," he said.

"Why not?"

"Cause he growls."

"Then take your doll," his mother said.

"I can't," he said again.

"Why not?"

"The doll cries."

The mother finally gave in and let the child come to bed with her and her husband until he fell asleep, then she carried him to his own room. From this she learned that even though the child's world is different from the one his parents perceive, to him it's quite real. Whereas a parent is apt to think the child is making up stories, to the child these fantasies, these friends that no one else can see, really exist.

Don't Give Too Much for the Whistle

Benjamin Franklin, eighteenth-century politician and one of the great American statesmen, once responded to a woman who had written to him about her ideas of paradise.

He agreed with her views and also about what needs to be done to get there. But he added that he felt it was even more important to worry about what happened here, now, and let the rest take care of itself when the time came.

His own experiences in life had taught him that many people were unhappy simply because their expectations were so much greater than the reality. Then he went on to give an example.

At the age of seven, he went with his family to visit some relatives in another town. His aunt and uncle, wanting him to have a good time, put some money in his pocket. Young Ben couldn't wait to go out and find a toy to spend it on.

On the way to the store he saw another boy sauntering along the road, blowing on a whistle. The shrill, high-pitched sound delighted him. This was just the toy he wanted.

"Here, you can have all my money for that whistle," he said to the boy. The offer was quickly accepted; money and whistle changed hands.

He ran all the way home, anxious to show off his purchase to the family. Proudly he strutted from room to room, whistle in mouth, piercing the air with noise. He made sure everyone got a thorough demonstration.

"How much did you pay for it?" they asked.

"All the money I had," he said.

His siblings and cousins howled with laughter. "You paid four times too much," they informed him gleefully. To make matters worse, they proceeded to cite all the other things he could have bought with the rest of the money. He got the point, and never again could he look at the whistle without feeling miserable.

This experience symbolized for him a very important lesson, which he later captured in the saying, "Don't give too much for the whistle."

Over and over throughout his life, Franklin said, he had observed various categories of people all too willing to pay too much for too little. Some, for instance, spent all their time courting the favor of whoever they thought could advance their position in life. They were the politicians who wanted to get ahead so badly that they let themselves get caught up in shifty political dealings. They didn't realize that in giving up their integrity, they lost everything they set out to gain.

He met people so preoccupied with their appearance that they spent a fortune to dress up like peacocks, always trying to be something they were not. Others wasted their time and money in pursuit of pleasure, partying the nights away, eating and drinking to excess. He also saw misers who hoarded everything they could for themselves. With hearts turned to stone, they expended all their energy looking for ways to keep from sharing what life had given to them.

Franklin noted that, in their various quests for what they thought would make them happy, these people were miserable. They couldn't see that their expectations were out of synchronization with the reality of their goals. They gave far too much for the whistle.

A Gift of Vision

The child with the toy tiger, on the other hand, is paying just enough for the whistle. He has created a reality that makes him happy. His tiger comes alive to play games with him, never argues or criticizes, and is a perfect companion for that stage of his journey through life.

Perhaps it is his parents, anxious to convince him that his world of imagination is false, who are giving too much for the whistle. Having lost the ability to use their creative imagination to make their own world more beautiful, they begin to destroy it for the child. And sure enough, by the age of seven or eight, the child's happy world of fantasy has pretty well disappeared.

My daughter used to talk about her invisible playmates, too, and like most parents, I didn't take her seriously. Then one day, for just a brief moment, I saw one of them—a little fellow dressed in green clothing.

"Did you see something?" I asked her.

"Yep," she answered matter of factly.

"Well, what did you see?" I prodded. She not only described exactly what I had seen, but explained that he was one of the little people who took care of the plants around our home.

266

From that point on, I stopped making fun of her invisible friends. This glimpse into her world made me realize that the one who had paid too much for the whistle was her dear old dad.

Respect

An ECK initiate works as a psychiatric counselor at one of the Veterans Administration hospitals. One day, an old bum stumbled in off the street. A highly offensive odor clung to his shabby clothes, and his stale breath attested to his problem with alcohol. His presence was so distasteful that no one wanted to get near him, but they certainly couldn't turn him away. A staff member resolved the dilemma by calling the ECKist to inform her, "We're sending him to you. Yours is the office of last resort."

The ECKist, who must deal with troubled clients all day long, makes it a point to chant HU periodically throughout the day. This raises her consciousness and gives her the insight and perspective to be an instrument of the Holy Spirit, to help the people who come to her in whatever way the ECK sees fit. As she waited for the man to arrive at her office, she closed her eyes and quietly chanted HU.

Just the day before, she had met with a client who was a United States senator. Today, as the scruffy individual walked into her office, she knew that she must show him the same respect as she had shown the senator.

She greeted the man kindly and invited him to be seated. Then, very gently, she began to draw him out. In the course of their conversation, he admitted that he had been on the bottle for years. "Drinking has ruined my life," he said sadly. He now wanted to give it up and would be grateful for any help he could get.

She talked with him for quite a while, outlining a program that he could follow to help himself. Assured that the support he needed would be given, the man began to relax and open up. First he told her all about his past. Then, as he spoke of his hopes for the future, his expression softened and his eyes began to shine with the most beautiful light of love. By the time he left, the ECKist could see that a transformation had taken place in him. The man had taken the first step to change his life.

The love was able to come through simply because she had accorded him the respect that he, as Soul, deserved. She gave this regardless of the outer appearance which put everyone else off.

Church Dream

A High Initiate in ECK was raised in the Pentecostal church, which is a religion of strong fundamentalist beliefs. Following the practices of that faith, her father, a minister in the church, saw to it that she was "saved" at the age of seven. Those impressionable early years were very difficult for her. The fear of hell and damnation instilled in her by her parents brought recurring nightmares.

In the worst of these nightmares, a trumpet would sound before she made it through the gates of heaven, leaving her lost to eternal damnation. Finally, at the age of twenty-one, she said, "I've had enough. No more."

In college she took up the study of psychology. As part of her studies, she learned that she needed professional help to undo the fears that she still carried with her from her earlier religious training. She was in therapy for eight years.

During that time, around the early 1960s, she began

to get a strong inner nudge that made her feel something was lacking in her life. There was something she had to accomplish, and until she did, her life would be a failure. But what was it?

Week after week she visited the libraries, often traveling to neighboring towns. She spent many hours searching the shelves in the theology sections. Surely there must be a book that can give me some answers, she thought. But nothing she read led her to the truth she sought.

One night, in the mid-1960s, she dreamed that she was walking along a street lined with churches. She entered each one hopefully, seeking whatever information she could find. But she always came out disappointed; the truth she wanted was not there. Finally only one remained, a tabernacle. "Everything I'm looking for must be in here," she said. "If not, I have no more hope."

But even there she found nothing.

Dejected, she crossed the street and wandered across a meadow toward a wooded area. Off in the distance she saw a figure dressed in gleaming white coming toward her. As the person drew closer, she could see his face. Much later she would recognize him as the Mahanta, the Living ECK Master.

Here in the dream state, he reached out to embrace her. Suddenly she knew that what she had been looking for all her life was right here.

Meeting the Mahanta

This was the meeting with the Inner Master, which is an integral part of ECKANKAR.

There are two sides of the Master—the Outer Master and the Inner Master. Before we find the Outer Master, we have already found the Inner Master. Once the connection with the Inner Master is made, we find the outer path. Usually we don't remember the experience of meeting the Master in the Radiant body on the inner planes; all we know is that something begins to drive us in a certain direction, leading to the path of ECKANKAR.

When we come to the ECK path, we may stay on it or not—the choice is our own. Even if we don't stay on the path in this lifetime, we will in another. Often Soul is in no hurry on Its journey home to God. There is plenty of time in eternity.

In the late 1960s the woman found ECKANKAR, and the Mahanta taught her about divine love. As she filled herself with love, she was able to move through the initiations. Eventually she became a Higher Initiate, and today she is a Regional ECK Spiritual Aide. On the day she was asked to serve in that position, she realized this is what she was to accomplish in this lifetime. The number of years that it took her to reach the point where she was to find her vocation in ECK made no difference—Soul sets Its own pace on the path back home to God.

The Typing Assignments

One way the Holy Spirit gives the individual direction is through the ECK-Vidya, the ancient science of prophecy. It's also called the Golden-tongued Wisdom. This feature is not confined only to the path of ECK. People in other religions are acquainted with it too, but they are often unable to develop it into a skill for deeper understanding of their spiritual psychology.

An ECKist from California had a friend, a Catholic woman, who ran her own typing service. By advertising in out-of-state newspapers, she got much of her work through the mail. Recently she had gotten an inner urge to move back East to her childhood home. But since her business was pretty well established on the West Coast, she wasn't sure what to do.

All of a sudden she began to get a whole series of jobs from a writer who lived in her hometown, with prospects for a lot more work in the future. This gave her the answer she was looking for. She decided to make the move.

The woman's Catholic background and beliefs would not allow her to accept ECK. Yet she and the ECKist often discussed the spiritual principles around which all the religious teachings revolve. The ECKist used her friend's experience as an example of the Golden-tongued Wisdom. Using general terms, she explained that it was one way in which the Holy Spirit works in people's lives, to help them form their future.

Though the friend had felt the inner prompting to move back East, she questioned it, not knowing if she should trust it. The work that came to her from her hometown was the Holy Spirit's way of giving her an answer that she was able to recognize.

Hints from the ECK

The ECK does this for us constantly. Often we don't recognize it. An initiate who decided to go to an ECK seminar set a certain date to make her flight reservations, but when the day came, she forgot. Throughout the day, every time she went outside, she saw an airplane in the sky.

Planes fly overhead all the time, but she couldn't recall the last time she had noticed one. Yet on that particular day, they stood out in her consciousness. This was the ECK-Vidya, the Golden-tongued Wisdom, trying to remind her that she had to make reservations.

271

It finally got through while she was out for a drive. A particularly noisy plane caught her attention, and she leaned way over the steering wheel to watch it pass over. That's the fifth plane I've seen today, she thought. Why am I noticing all these planes? Then it hit her: the flight reservations.

It bothered her that it had taken five obvious hints before she finally caught on. She couldn't help wondering how many other times the ECK had told her something five times or more, and she hadn't heard.

Golden-tongued Wisdom

The ECKist often finds himself in this position on the journey home to God. As he goes from the First Initiation to the Second, the Third, and so on, the Mahanta is constantly testing him. But all too frequently the chela doesn't realize it. That's no problem. The Master will keep repeating the test until the chela finally recognizes it as such, until he sees that it is for his own spiritual edification.

The ECK-Vidya, the ancient science of prophecy, must be understood in its broadest interpretation. Not only does it deal with the future, as the word *prophecy* implies. More importantly, it also gives us deeper insight into the present. Sometimes it allows us to take a look into a past life, either through the dream state or through unconscious memories, to gain an understanding of a present condition.

Even if we do not recall the inner experience specifically, in some way the ECK will bring it to our attention. For example, words we are reading may appear to light up for us, perhaps surrounded by a golden light. In one way or another, it will come through to us in our daily life, for our own good. This is what I call the Golden-tongued Wisdom.

As we travel the path of ECK, the Mahanta does everything possible to make our life better—if we could but hear him. In time, the ECK initiations lead us to a greater awareness of the spiritual realities which occur around us every moment of every day.

Depth Gauge

An ECKist signed up for a weekly class in scuba diving. Everything went well until the day the instructor announced that he was taking the students out the following Saturday morning to test a new depth gauge. That night the Mahanta came to the ECKist in the dream state and made one single statement: "Don't be afraid to die."

The ECKist woke up terrified. Is this a test? he wondered. Since the only way to test a depth gauge is to dive fairly deep, is the Master testing me to see how courageous I am? On the other hand, he knows how thickheaded I can be. Could he be warning me not to go?

Don't be afraid to die. The statement bothered him all week long. He didn't know what to do. He only hoped the Mahanta would somehow clear up the question by Saturday.

Finally he made up his mind: He was going to take the test dive no matter what.

The instructor and students had arranged to meet at a specific place on Saturday morning. With tanks and fins, the ECKist arrived at the appointed time. He looked around for familiar faces and found only the instructor's. None of the other students had shown up.

"I'm not going out there with only one student," the instructor said. "We'll cancel the dive for now and do it some other time."

The ECKist realized then that the Golden-tongued Wisdom had spoken with startling clarity. "The Master knows how thick my understanding is sometimes," he said later. "When he couldn't get through to me, he probably went to the other ten scuba divers and said, 'Don't be afraid to die.'"

Polishing a Manuscript

I recently completed the book *Soul Travelers of the Far Country*. It tells of my experiences with Rebazar Tarzs and Peddar Zaskq, and also the events that led up to 1981, when I accepted the Rod of ECK Power.

It took a long time to write the book. Not only was I kept busy working on discourses and articles, but there were ongoing administrative and organizational considerations that required attention. And besides all that, writing is very difficult. I wanted to take the time I needed to put my best into it.

You are probably familiar with one of Colleen McCullough's most successful books, *The Thorn Birds,* which was later made into a TV miniseries. The author once revealed that she had to rewrite each book up to ten times before she got it to come out exactly the way she wanted. I was very impressed when I read that. I do pretty much the same thing.

I began the manuscript for *Soul Travelers of the Far Country* in the spring of 1983, completing the first draft in a mere forty days. This past winter I dug it out of the drawer to polish it up one last time, certain that it just needed a little touch-up here and there. But after reading it over, my heart sank. "I can't use this," I said. Some parts could be kept in, but basically, the whole book had to be rewritten. Luckily I've adapted myself to the computer age, so the revisions went much faster than in the days when I used only a typewriter.

The next step was to run it through the editorial team at the ECK Office. After they went over the manuscript, they returned it to me so I could weigh their recommendations—which meant I had to go through the whole thing still another time.

Another project has been converting my talks into readable form for the Mahanta Transcripts series. We are working with certain people in the field who have a particular talent for extracting the written word from the spoken.

The Lost Transcript

Recently I sent a transcript of a past talk to one of the individuals who will be working on it before it goes to the office editorial team. She took it with her to the 1987 ECKANKAR Creative Arts Festival in Chicago, planning to get started on it between other seminar activities.

One afternoon she attached the transcript to a clipboard and placed a few sheets of blank paper on top of it so that no one could see what she was carrying around. She sat down in the hotel lounge, ordered a diet Coke, and got to work. Pretty soon an old woman in a raggedy coat came over and asked her for a dollar. The ECKist set the clipboard down on a table and took some money out of her purse. As soon as the old woman left, the ECKist glanced at her watch and realized that she had to get over to the seminar registration desk, where she had volunteered to work that afternoon. She jumped up and hurried back to the seminar.

Only later did it occur to her that she had forgotten the clipboard. Assuming the waitress would have set it aside until someone came back to claim it, she rushed back to the lounge and asked the bartender about it.

"I threw it out," he said. "Didn't look important."

She couldn't believe her ears. "But there was a typed manuscript with notes clipped to it," she pointed out. "It's not like it was a crumpled-up napkin. Why would you throw it away?"

He merely shrugged his shoulders and turned away. She stared at him for a moment, trying to imagine the scene: he picks up the clipboard, sees several typed sheets of paper, says, "This must be junk," and tosses it in the garbage.

"Where do you keep the garbage?" she asked. "Maybe I can find it."

"Too late," he said with the utmost unconcern. "The garbage has been picked up."

She went to the front desk and explained the situation to a clerk. "Can you tell me where I can find the garbage that was picked up from the lounge?"

"I'm afraid not," the clerk said.

Figuring it must still be on the hotel premises, she called the person in charge of maintenance and told him what had happened. "It's very important that I find it," she explained.

"If it's in the garbage, it's gone," he said. "Sorry I can't help you."

"Then please tell me who can," she persisted.

A few minutes later she got a call from the assistant manager of the hotel and told the story all over again. Of course, she didn't present the problem to him the way she saw it—that the Master had entrusted this transcript to her, she had lost it, and now she would do everything in her power to get it back. Nevertheless, he must have sensed her determination.

"Just tell me where to find the garbage, and I'll go through it myself," she said.

Seeing that he couldn't talk her out of it, the assistant manager of this large hotel in Chicago resigned himself to the fact that he was going to have to rummage through the garbage. Fortunately, she said, he was too much of a gentleman to let her do it herself.

They entered the freight elevator and descended into the bowels of the hotel. He then led the way through the dark, dungeon-like basement to a foul-smelling room. There the garbage was piled several feet deep in a huge dumpster.

With only a pair of knee-high boots to protect his natty tan suit, the assistant manager bravely jumped down into the dumpster. "He was so cute, I fell in love right there," the ECKist said later. She jumped in to join him. Together they spent the next half hour digging through scores of plastic bags full of putrid garbage. But the transcript was nowhere to be found.

Finally they gave up the search. They went back upstairs and walked through the lobby, smelling like skunks, looking like they had just crawled out of, well, a garbage can. She thanked him for his help and headed to her room to clean up.

Suddenly she had a feeling that because she had made the effort, a miracle would occur: someone would have found the transcript, and it would be there waiting for her. Anxiously she opened the door, entered the room, looked around, and—it wasn't there.

She had recently finished working on an earlier talk in which I told the story "A Message to Garcia." During the Spanish-American War, President McKinley wanted to send an urgent message to General Garcia in Cuba, but there was no way to get it to him. One of his aides said, "There is only one person who can do it, and his name is

Rowan." Rowan accepted the impossible mission, first traveling by boat, then creeping on foot through the jungle. When he finally emerged over two weeks later, the message had been delivered. Everybody knew that only Rowan could have done it.

The ECKist had tried to do everything she thought Rowan would have done. But it didn't turn out the way she expected. In the end, all she could do was write to the ECK Office and very sheepishly say, "I lost the transcript. Please send me another copy. I'll guard this one with my life."

Learning Love

She didn't realize it yet, but obstacles like this are par for the course. They occur in any endeavor to present the ECK message to the world.

But as you attempt to overcome the obstacles, you are gaining in spiritual growth. First you learn patience, and finally you learn love. And love, after all, is the heart of the ECK teachings. If we can love, we can have all. With the love of God come the attributes of God: wisdom, power, and freedom.

A spiritual upliftment occurs for each person who is able to make it to an ECK seminar, and most of you will recognize it in the days and weeks to come. Wherever I go, I see Souls who are looking for the message of the Light and Sound of God. Within them is the impulse to seek what they need to find their way back home. My job is that of a messenger—to bring into words whatever I can to inspire you and show you the way. But even though you are given the inspiration and shown the way, it still remains for you to walk the path to God yourself. No one else can do it for you.

I wish each of you a safe journey on the path back home to God.

ECKANKAR European Seminar, The Hague, The Netherlands
Sunday, July 19, 1987

Heaven and hell are not different places but different states of consciousness. The state you are in depends on your experience, or vice versa, at any particular time.

16

A Co-worker with the Mahanta

I'm very happy to be at this seminar here in Africa. I know that many of you traveled great distances and went through personal hardships to make the journey to Abidjan and share the message of ECK with us. But the blessings that will come to you for making the effort will repay you many times over.

Telephone Call

After we left the ECKANKAR European Seminar last weekend, we stopped off in Geneva for a meeting. Not even the Higher Initiates knew of my plans to be at the meeting; it hadn't been mentioned on the invitations that were sent out to the initiates. Even so, many people made a special effort to be there.

An ECKist who lived several hours away from Geneva had not planned to come to the meeting. But that morning he saw his two-year-old son playing with the telephone. "Who are you talking to?" he asked jokingly.

"Harji," the boy said.

Harji is an affectionate nickname of mine. The father, a very aware individual, didn't hesitate for a moment. He immediately changed his plans, went out and bought a train ticket to Geneva, and came down with his son. They were standing outside of the hotel when I arrived. "I'm very grateful to my son," he said. "He gave me the message that you'd be here."

Masters-in-Training

The title of this talk is "A Co-worker with the Mahanta." It refers to a person in training for ECK Mastership. One who gives of himself to bring the message of ECK to others is acting as a Co-worker with the Mahanta. As you become perfected in this capacity, you rise in states of consciousness to one day become a Co-worker with God.

A Co-worker with God, then, is one who has reached the state of God-Realization and fully understands his spiritual relationship with the SUGMAD.

The little boy on the telephone was being a Co-worker with the Mahanta.

Enthusiasm

During the meeting in Geneva, I asked the ECK initiates if they had any questions. A mother holding a little girl just under two years of age told me about a dream she'd had recently. On the inner planes, the Inner Master was talking to her about her daughter. Just before the dream ended, Wah Z had said, "It's too much for her." The mother wondered if I could tell her what this meant.

I looked at the little girl for a moment. Though born into an ECK family in this lifetime, I could see that the child had come from another religion. Her mother was so enthusiastic about ECK and emitted such strong energies that the child was not able to withstand them.

I explained to the woman that her daughter needed a life of peace and quiet, and suggested that she devote more attention to the welfare of the family. Only in that way could the child grow up to become strong in ECK.

After the talk I went to the back of the room to greet some of the ECKists, and the mother came up to say hello. The little girl respectfully stood several feet back, lost in the crowd of adults. Her mother said that the child wanted to come over and thank me for the answer I had given.

Remembering herself as a grownup, the little girl waited for someone to lift her up so she could be as tall as I. Very gently we touched cheeks. She was not even two years of age, but as we looked at each other I knew she understood that I was watching out for her spiritual welfare. When she was set back down on the floor, she walked away in a very dignified manner and returned to her mother's side.

Heaven and Hell

The room in Geneva was very hot. Though it was heavenly to be with the ECK initiates, the heat was quite hellish. It seemed a fitting time to discuss how their feelings about heaven and hell had changed since they came into ECK.

Some still envisioned a heaven as it is described in the Bible, a place of high stone walls embedded with jewels, where the inhabitants wear long robes and serene expressions. But a few of them thought of the people in heaven as being without any real enjoyment.

To explain heaven and hell as states of consciousness rather than actual places, I used this analogy:

Imagine that you are at a game preserve where the animals can roam about in their natural habitat. It is a

283

beautiful park setting. Here and there you see visitors strolling among the animals. You watch as the zebras, giraffes, elephants, lions, and tigers move leisurely through the tall grass, on their way to a watering hole with crystal-clear blue water. There are buildings nearby where one can go for shelter if an animal becomes vicious. That seems unlikely, for the scene you are observing on the inner planes is peaceful and tranquil.

This is heaven.

At this point an elephant looks over and sees you standing there. Suddenly it charges toward you. Panicked, you turn and head for the shelter. But the building is far enough away to make you question whether you can get there before the elephant gets to you. Desperately you race for your life. The huge animal pounds closer and closer, steadily gaining ground. Now you are only steps away from being stomped on.

This is hell.

Just in the nick of time, you make it to the stone building. Sweating and winded, you slam the heavy door shut behind you. You are safely inside now; the danger has passed. You calm down as you realize how fortunate you are. And very soon you are back in heaven.

So heaven and hell are not different places but different states of consciousness. The state you are in depends upon your experience, or vice versa, at any particular time.

Out-of-Body Experience

Our first visits to the inner planes are usually made in the dream state. Occasionally people are fortunate enough to begin with conscious Soul Travel, sometimes even before they come in contact with the teachings of ECK.

A Second Initiate wrote to me about an experience he had twelve years ago. This was long before he ever heard of Paul Twitchell, ECKANKAR, or the spiritual travelers. While a soldier stationed at a military base, he often found himself out of the body at night, walking through walls. He thought this a fantastic adventure. At other times he got out of the body but didn't go anywhere, yet had the special ability to see through walls and lockers in which clothing was stored.

But despite all of his initial out-of-the-body experiences, he made an interesting observation: After he got his Second Initiation, he no longer Soul traveled. He describes his present state as one in which "I see, I know, I am."

He is speaking of the "I" consciousness of the Soul Plane. Soul Travel is a fast method of moving into the higher worlds, but an individual whose consciousness becomes firmly established on the Soul Plane no longer requires the sense of movement. His perceptions are more immediate and direct.

Even though we begin the path of ECK with dreams and then progress to Soul Travel, the day will come when we must give up Soul Travel. This is when we move into the spiritual state of consciousness, which puts us in the state of seeing, knowing, and being.

The ECKist Minister

As the teachings of ECK move out into the world, many people still in their old religions hear about it. They wonder if they should make a change and begin to study ECK. The decision becomes much more difficult if the person who finds ECK is a minister who must support his family.

A thirteen-year-old boy, whose uncle is a Higher

Initiate in ECK, sometimes went to church with his parents. Because the boy was familiar with ECK through his uncle, he couldn't help noticing that the minister was actually weaving many ECK principles into his sermons. He wondered if he should talk to the minister about it. He discussed it with his uncle, who thought it was a good idea.

One Sunday after the services, the teenager approached the minister and told him a little bit about the path of ECK. The minister was intrigued. He said he had been having experiences with the Light during his prayers and meditations, but nothing in his religion could explain what was happening to him. When he asked more questions than the boy could answer, the boy offered to put him in touch with his uncle.

The Higher Initiate met with the minister and explained more about the Sound and Light of ECK. He also told him about HU, a sacred name for God. Though the minister needed his job to take care of his family, he recognized the validity of the ECK teachings. In time he came to view himself as an instrument of the Mahanta. The minister came to believe his real job was to introduce his congregation to the principles of the Sound and Light of God.

The minister sponsored a new program—a special comparative religion class where people from other religions were encouraged to come and speak about their teachings. He often invited the Higher Initiate to share the teachings of ECK. These classes, held once a month, were usually attended by the more spiritually advanced members of the congregation who were willing to reach out for greater awareness. Over a period of time, as they became ready for the higher teachings, they were able to make the step onto the ECK path through the minister, who was acting as a Co-worker with the Mahanta.

Into the White Light

Another example of being a Co-worker with the Mahanta involves an ECKist who worked as a fireman. One evening the initiate reported to work at the fire station to relieve the captain. But instead of leaving at the end of his shift, the captain felt a strong need to stay and talk to the ECKist about something that was troubling him.

A short time ago, he said, his elderly father suffered a heart attack. The shock of it caused his mother to have a mild stroke. While she was hospitalized to determine the extent of the damage done by the stroke, the tests uncovered an even more serious condition. If his mother survived, her condition would be very painful for a long period of time.

The captain had been very close to his parents all his life, and now he was faced with the possibility of losing both of them.

"Since you are so close to your mother, could you handle it if she were to die?" the ECKist asked.

"If it would spare her months or even years of pain, yes," the captain said. "I just wish she wouldn't have to suffer."

They talked a while longer, then the captain went home and left the ECKist to finish out his shift. When no fires were reported over the next few hours, he stretched out on his cot to relax and soon fell asleep.

Suddenly he awoke in the higher worlds and found himself in conversation with the captain and an elderly woman. "This is my mother," the captain said. Before them was a brilliant white light. The older woman seemed drawn to it. Turning to her son, she gave him a long look filled with affection. "Good-bye," she said and began to move toward the light.

The two men walked along with her, but as they got closer, the light became too strong for the captain. "I can't go any farther," he said to the ECKist. "Would you go with my mother?" The ECK initiate, as a Co-worker with the Mahanta, proceeded with his friend's mother into the brilliant white light.

Somebody woke him up to tell him that the captain had just called the station. He wanted to let them know that his mother had died during the night. This came as no surprise to the ECKist, of course. He knew it meant the woman had finished working out a certain type of karma, so there was no need for her to undergo months of suffering. At the same time, he knew that the Mahanta had given him the opportunity to escort a Soul across the borders to a greater life.

This is one of the services that an initiate in ECK learns to perform as a Co-worker with the Mahanta. Someday you, too, will do these things, and greater.

I wish you the blessings of the SUGMAD and I give you my love. Safe passage on your journey home to God.

ECK African Seminar, Abidjan, Ivory Coast,
July 25, 1987

Glossary of ECKANKAR Terms

Words set in SMALL CAPS are defined elsewhere in the Glossary.

ARAHATA. An experienced and qualified teacher for ECKANKAR classes.

CHELA. A spiritual student.

ECK. The Life Force, the Holy Spirit, or Audible Life Current which sustains all life.

ECKANKAR. Religion of the Light and Sound of God. Also known as the Ancient Science of SOUL TRAVEL. A truly spiritual religion for the individual in modern times, known as the secret path to God via dreams and Soul Travel. The teachings provide a framework for anyone to explore their own spiritual experiences. Established by Paul Twitchell, the modern-day founder, in 1965.

ECK MASTERS. Spiritual Masters who can assist and protect people in their spiritual studies and travels. The ECK Masters are from a long line of God-Realized Souls who know the responsibility that goes with spiritual freedom.

HU. The secret name for God. The singing of the word HU, pronounced like the man's name Hugh, is considered a love song to God. It is sung in the ECK Worship Service.

INITIATION. Earned by the ECK member through spiritual unfoldment and service to God. The initiation is a private ceremony in which the individual is linked to the Sound and Light of God.

LIVING ECK MASTER. The title of the spiritual leader of ECKANKAR. His duty is to lead Souls back to God. The Living ECK Master can assist spiritual students physically as the Outer Master, in the dream state as the Dream Master, and in the spiritual worlds as the Inner Master. Sri Harold Klemp became the Living ECK Master in 1981.

MAHANTA. A title to describe the highest state of God Consciousness on earth, often embodied in the LIVING ECK MASTER. He is the Living Word.

289

PLANES. The levels of heaven, such as the Astral, Causal, Mental, Etheric, and Soul planes.

SATSANG. A class in which students of ECK study a monthly lesson from ECKANKAR.

THE SHARIYAT-KI-SUGMAD. The sacred scriptures of ECKANKAR. The scriptures are comprised of twelve volumes in the spiritual worlds. The first two were transcribed from the inner planes by Paul Twitchell, modern-day founder of ECKANKAR.

SOUL. The True Self. The inner, most sacred part of each person. Soul exists before birth and lives on after the death of the physical body. As a spark of God, Soul can see, know, and perceive all things. It is the creative center of Its own world.

SOUL TRAVEL. The expansion of consciousness. The ability of Soul to transcend the physical body and travel into the spiritual worlds of God. Soul Travel is taught only by the Living ECK Master. It helps people unfold spiritually and can provide proof of the existence of God and life after death.

SOUND AND LIGHT OF ECK. The Holy Spirit. The two aspects through which God appears in the lower worlds. People can experience them by looking and listening within themselves and through Soul Travel.

SPIRITUAL EXERCISES OF ECK. The daily practice of certain techniques to get us in touch with the Light and Sound of God.

SUGMAD. A sacred name for God. SUGMAD is neither masculine nor feminine; IT is the source of all life.

WAH Z. The spiritual name of Sri Harold Klemp. It means the Secret Doctrine. It is his name in the spiritual worlds.

Index

293

Government, 55, 117
Grace, 84, 156
Grandfather, 67–69
Grateful-dove story, 114–15
Gratitude, 180, 225, 226, 283
 of animals, 114–15, 169
 to ECK, 167
 meaning of, 82
 to others, 76, 206, 267
 power of, 219–20, 247,
  249–50
Great-aunt story, 235–37
Greed, 2, 16, 265–66
Greece (Greeks), 78, 79, 100,
 187
Ground-squirrel story,
 152–53
Growth, 72, 172, 278
Guidance, 42, 46–47, 117,
 140, 151, 213, 256
Guilt(y), 73, 83, 110

Habit(s), 71, 100, 116, 117,
 163, 225, 229, 258
Happiness, 16, 94, 177, 239
 of others, 10, 76, 108–9
 place of, 105–6, 119
 ultimate, 50
 what gives you, 73, 110,
  211, 266
Hardship(s), 137, 143, 153,
 192, 215, 240, 247, 258,
 281
Harji, 281
Harm, 97, 205, 232
Harmony, 76, 154, 155
Hawk, 124, 125
Hazing, 155–56
Headaches, 29–30, 41–43
Healer, 42, 43, 189
Healing(s), 6, 40, 245. *See
 also* Chiropractor(s);
 Doctor(s); Nutrition(ist);
 Veterinarian(s)
 by the ECK, 45, 120, 123,
  190
 from effects of passions, 16
 from inner music, 184

instant, 244, 245
and karma, 117
from loneliness, 23
miracles, 25, 44, 188
process of, 31–32
psychic, 41–42
receiving a, 11, 27
request for a, 42–43
spiritual, 12, 26, 44, 113,
 116, 122, 189
Health
 better, 24, 72
 good spiritual, 114
 ill, 4–5, 29
 problems, 32, 72, 126, 287
 vision and, 27–29
Heart(s)
 attack, 180, 287
 golden, 62
 loving, 77, 82, 226
 open, 191, 192, 208, 219,
  220, 247
 truth contained in, 172
 turned to stone, 266
 understanding, 224
Heartbreak, 126, 239, 244
Heat, 121, 283
Heaven(s)
 experiences in, 16, 180
 facts about, 38, 283–84
 gates of, 268
 must be rewon, 71
 third, 101
 as the unknown, 73, 148
 walk the, 36
Hell, 9, 31, 235, 268, 283–84
Help(ing)
 animals, 76, 114, 204
 asking for, 21, 85, 178, 189,
  205, 210, 213, 244
 from discourses, 144
 in dream state, 162
 from ECK, 73, 189
 from Mahanta, 39, 65–67
 medical, 27, 40, 189
 others, 60, 68, 76, 185, 188,
  267–68
 professional, 183, 184

299

301

Love *(continued)*
  is all, 83, 84, 157
  learning, 77, 80, 169–70,
    213, 219, 245, 278
  and life, 78, 216
  others, 244, 245, 267–68
  replaces fear, 157, 210
  replaces karma, 61, 209
  transcends death, 49
  what you do, 191
  yourself, 212–13
Lust, 2, 16
Lying, 171, 228, 245

McCullough, Colleen, 274
MacLaine, Shirley, 180
Mahanta. *See also* Inner
    Master; Wah Z
  asking the, 211–12
  and chela, 68, 187, 192, 218,
    219, 248, 272, 273
  face of the, 85, 269
  hand(s) of, 205, 233
  is highest consciousness,
    247
  meeting, 269–70
  message from, 60, 226, 253
  presence of, 6, 116
  protection of. *See* Protec-
    tion: of the Mahanta
  surrender to, 76, 210, 215
Mahanta Transcripts series,
    275–78
Manifestation(s), 13, 185, 192.
    See also ECK: manifesta-
    tions of
Manuscript, 46–47, 214–15,
    275–78
Marriage, 48, 191, 209, 213
Master(s). *See also* ECK
    Master(s); Inner Master;
    Living ECK Master;
    Mahanta; Outer Master
  how a, works, 134
  in name of, 206
  two sides of, 269–70
  works with spiritual
    student, 15, 101, 148,

186, 229
Mather, Cotton, 245–46
Medicine, 139, 190
Meditations, 286
Meeting(s), 1, 2, 3, 211, 281
  with Mahanta, 269–70
Memory (memories), 29, 148,
    192, 272. *See also*
    Plane(s): Causal
Mental
  body. *See* Body (bodies):
    Mental
  clarity, 16
  exercises, 247
  Plane. *See* Plane(s): Mental
  processes, 162
Message
  carry ECK, 60, 181, 278
  from the ECK, 47, 167, 175
  of ECK, 101, 194, 216, 243,
    246, 281–82
  to Garcia, 277–78
Military, 155, 179, 285
Milo of Crotona, 186–87
Mind, 10, 126, 189, 190, 193,
    210, 211, 249. *See also*
    Mental
Minister, 22, 46, 188, 204,
    212, 245–46, 268, 285–86
Minnesota, 25, 131, 132, 149,
    224
  Chanhassen, 180, 181
Miracle(s), 25, 26, 44, 150,
    188, 189, 190, 277
Mirror story, 151
Mission(s), 31, 50, 91, 151,
    236, 278
Missionary, 27
Mistake, 108
Mock, 157
Monastery, 238, 258–59. *See
    also* Katsupari Monas-
    tery
Money. *See also* Earning:
    money
  asking for, 225–26
  paying, 105, 109, 138, 152,
    206, 265

302

problems, 3, 32, 80, 126, 220
Monkey(s), 148
  hundredth, 160–62
Motivation, 3, 73, 92, 157, 162
Mountain world, 238
Moving, 44, 94, 213, 233, 234, 271
  to Minnesota, 131, 149
Ms. Pac-Man, 137
Music(ian), 59–60, 190–92
  inner, 159, 183–85
  rock, 93–94
  tone-deaf, 77
Mystery schools, 79, 98–100
Mystic World, The 10
Myths, 171

Need(s), 22, 136, 137, 235, 248
Negative power(s), 94, 119. *See also* Kal Niranjan
Negotiations, 154–55
New Orleans, 61
Newspaper-vendor story, 113–14
New Zealand, 90
Nightmares, 205, 215, 268
Noise, 94
Nuclear weapons, 190
Nudge(s), 59, 60, 96, 175, 197, 269, 270–71, 272
Nurse, 251
Nutrition(ist), 72, 172–75

Observing, 72, 134, 161, 285
Obstacle(s), 73, 80, 138, 142, 278. *See also* Problem(s)
Ocean of Love and Mercy, 103. *See also* SUGMAD
Opinion(s), 120, 167
Opportunity (opportunities), 58, 77, 103, 109, 148, 251
Order of the Vairagi ECK Masters. *See* ECK Master(s)
Ott, John, 27–29
Outer Master, 6, 11, 269
Out-of-body experiences, 59, 60, 179–80. *See also* Body (bodies): leaving the; Soul Travel
Overweight, 211–13, 223

Pace, 66, 158
Pain(s), 26, 29, 30, 76, 247, 250, 287
Pandora's box, 2
Panhandler story, 225–26
Parkinson's disease, 139
Passions of the mind, 16, 138, 158. *See also* Anger; Attachment; Greed; Lust; Vanity
Past
  cleaning up, 123
  life (lives), 17–18, 64, 91, 93, 162, 163, 238, 244, 272
  trauma, 210
Path(s)
  of ECK, 27, 42, 94, 96, 97, 192, 214, 229, 247, 254, 273
  inner-directed, 127
  of love, 94, 96, 103
  middle, 96
  progress on, 61, 125, 127, 143, 285
  spiritual, 94, 229, 245, 256
  trying other, 110
  walk the, 147, 278
Patience, 55, 109, 205, 212, 239, 278
Peace, 118, 283
Pebble, white, 169
Peddar Zaskq, 162, 192, 212, 238, 274. *See also* Twitchell, Paul
Perception(s), 16, 114, 285
Perfection, 6, 79, 83, 247–48, 282
Perspective, 84, 231, 267
Pets, 22–25, 40, 168–70
Philosophy, 78, 85
Photographer, 210–11
Plane(s)
  Astral, 11, 12, 15, 30, 68,

303

304

groups, 46, 97
space, 95–96, 155, 157, 236–37
Psychology, 228, 268, 270
Purification, 159, 250
Puzzle box, Chinese, 1–3, 16, 18
Pythagoras, 78, 79, 98, 99

Quaker, 113–14
Question(s)
  answer(s) to, 7, 13, 74–75, 82, 152–53, 213, 271, 282–83, 286
  in contemplation, 32, 47, 84, 126–27
  from Higher Initiates. *See* Higher Initiate(s): questions from
  not, 172, 226
  spiritual, 248, 251
  why things happen, 174–75

Radio, 95, 228
Rami Nuri, 10
React(ion), 99, 100, 118
  to others, 36, 114
Realization(s), 16, 63, 123, 174, 226, 240
  God-. *See* God-Realization
  Self-. *See* Self-Realization
Rebazar Tarzs, 84, 103, 192, 212, 238, 274
Rebellion, 82–83
Regional ECK Spiritual Aide, 256, 270
Reincarnation, 209. *See also* Past: life (lives)
Relationship(s), 247. *See also* Family (families): relationships
  love, 209, 217
  old, 208–10
  problems, 29–30, 32, 82, 126, 213
  with self, 256
Relax(ation), 73, 208, 268, 287

Religion(s), 235, 270. *See also* Christian(ity); Church(es)
  coming from another, 282
  experiences in, 22, 135, 158, 218, 251
  freedom of, 219
  heavens in different, 16
  starting a, 194
Renovation, 185–86, 196
Repentance, 43, 195
Resentment, 30, 82
Respect, 75, 223, 268
Responsibility(ies), 194. *See also* Action(s): responsibility for
  accepting, 36, 195
  as citizens, 75
  freedom and, 18, 95
  not your, 226
  self-, 36, 195, 245
Resurrection, 171–72
Restaurant(s), 28, 180, 185–86, 230
Reunion story, 67–69
Rituals, 100
River-run story, 65–67
Road, rough, 124–25
Rod of ECK Power, 274
Role, 40, 119, 252, 256
Routine(s), 87, 259
Rubber-duck story, 210, 211
Rules, 54, 56, 57, 87, 228
Russia, 154

Sadness, 50, 244
Saint Paul, 101, 160
Salem witch trials, 9, 16–18
Salvation, 268
Santa Claus, 171
Satan, 31
Satsang. *See* ECKANKAR: Satsang classes
School, 16–18. *See also* Education
  attendance, 137, 253–54
  counselor, 216–19
  first day of, 36–38
  religious, 156

305

of buzzing insects, 159
of a choir, 252
of crickets, 251
of ECK, 48–49, 159, 251–52
experiences with, 48, 225
of falling rain, 251
of flute, 48, 251, 252
of music, 159
of nature, 224
of water, 48
of whistle, 48, 264–65
Sound Current, 159, 178, 184
Spirit (Divine). *See also* ECK;
  Holy Spirit
  how, works, 27, 47, 149,
    151, 183, 253
  proof of, 44
  ways of, 46, 48, 175
Spiritual
  betterment, 247, 251
  blockages, 120, 125
  breakthrough, 7
  character, 12
  excellence, 117
  exercises. *See* Spiritual
    Exercises of ECK
  heritage, 49–50
  hierarchy, 135
  lag, 214
  liberation, 152
  quality, 141
  stamina, 98
  traveler(s), 179, 187, 193,
    285
  unfoldment. *See* Unfold-
    ment: spiritual
  welfare, 8, 283
Spiritual Exercises of ECK,
  12
  benefits of, 91, 119, 126,
    160, 162
  and consciousness, 32, 84,
    101, 147
  experiences with, 62
  experimenting with, 90, 109
  give strength, 30, 260
  and HU, 163, 243
  for practical people, 21, 125

regular practice of, 27, 72,
    102, 120, 205
  and Soul Travel, 16, 214–15
Spiritual Eye, 10
Spiritualists, 97
Spirituality, 135, 155, 192
Spiritual Notebook, The, 160
Spiritual Services, 143
Stability, 66
Stand up for yourself, 75, 96
Store-proprietor story, 57–58
"Storm Got Bigger, The," 128
Story (stories)
  examples in, 27, 144, 195,
    243, 257
  making up, 171, 264
  moral of, 199–200
  needs conflict, 2, 54–55,
    58–59
  telling, 17, 104, 152, 161,
    277
Strength, 47, 123, 156, 167,
    186–87, 188, 204, 259,
    283
Stress(es), 3, 4, 186
Success, 32, 74, 125, 127, 164,
    210, 215
Suffering, 77, 82, 151, 205,
    287–88
SUGMAD, 103, 172, 177,
    247
Superstition, 189
Support, 268
Surrender
  ability to, 211
  act of, 80, 177, 213
  blocks to, 210
  to ECK, 42, 64, 69, 141,
    206, 212
  and karma, 204, 215
  technique for, 219
  true, 85
Survival, 67, 72, 73, 92, 157,
    177
Sweet potatoes, 160–61
Symbol(s), 99, 125, 143, 160,
    230
Sympathy, 151, 157

307

309

How to Learn More about ECKANKAR
Religion of the Light and Sound of God

Why are you as important to God as any famous head of state, priest, minister, or saint that ever lived?

- Do you know God's purpose in your life?
- Why does God's Will seem so unpredictable?
- Why do you talk to God, but practice no one religion?

ECKANKAR can show you why special attention from God is neither random nor reserved for the few known saints. But it is for every individual. It is for anyone who opens himself to Divine Spirit, the Light and Sound of God.

People want to know the secrets of life and death. In response to this need Sri Harold Klemp, today's spiritual leader of ECKANKAR, and Paul Twitchell, its modern-day founder, have written a series of monthly discourses that give the Spiritual Exercises of ECK. They can lead Soul in a direct way to God.

Those who wish to study ECKANKAR can receive these special monthly discourses which give clear, simple instructions for the spiritual exercises.

Membership in ECKANKAR Includes

1. Twelve monthly discourses which include information on Soul, the spiritual meaning of dreams, Soul Travel techniques, and ways to establish a personal relationship with Divine Spirit. You may study them alone at home or in a class with others.
2. The *Mystic World,* a quarterly newsletter with a Wisdom Note and articles by the Living ECK Master. In it are also letters and articles from students of ECKANKAR around the world.
3. Special mailings to keep you informed of upcoming ECKANKAR seminars and activities worldwide, new study materials available from ECKANKAR, and more.
4. The opportunity to attend ECK Satsang classes and book discussions with others in your community.
5. Initiation eligibility.
6. Attendance at certain meetings for members of ECKANKAR at ECK seminars.

How to Find Out More

To request membership in ECKANKAR using your credit card (or for a free booklet on membership) call (612) 544-0066, weekdays, between 8 a.m. and 5 p.m., central time. Or write to: ECKANKAR, Att: Information, P.O. Box 27300, Minneapolis, MN 55427 U.S.A.

Introductory Books on ECKANKAR

How to Find God, Mahanta Transcripts, Book 2
Harold Klemp

Learn how to recognize and interpret the guidance each of us is *already receiving* from Divine Spirit in day-to-day events—for inner freedom, love, and guidance from God. The author gives spiritual exercises to uplift physical, emotional, mental, and spiritual health as well as a transforming sound called *HU,* which can be sung for inner upliftment.

The Secret Teachings, Mahanta Transcripts, Book 3
Harold Klemp

If you're interested in the secret, yet practical knowledge of the Vairagi ECK Masters, this book will fascinate and inspire you. Discover how to apply the unique Spiritual Exercises of ECK—dream exercises, visualizations, and Soul Travel methods—to unlock your natural abilities as Soul. Learn how to hear the little-known sounds of God and follow Its Light for practical daily guidance.

ECKANKAR—The Key to Secret Worlds
Paul Twitchell

This introduction to Soul Travel features simple, half-hour spiritual exercises to help you become more aware of yourself as Soul—divine, immortal, and free. You'll learn step-by-step how to unravel the secrets of life from a Soul point of view: your unique destiny or purpose in this life; how to make personal contact with the God Force, Spirit; and the hidden causes at work in your everyday life—all using the ancient art of Soul Travel.

The Tiger's Fang, Paul Twitchell
Paul Twitchell's teacher, Rebazar Tarzs, takes him on a journey through vast worlds of Light and Sound, to sit at the feet of the spiritual Masters. Their conversations bring out the secret of how to draw closer to God—and awaken Soul to Its spiritual destiny. Many have used this book, with its vivid descriptions of heavenly worlds and citizens, to begin their own spiritual adventures.

For fastest service, phone (612) 544-0066 weekdays between 8 a.m. and 5 p.m., central time, to request books using your credit card, or look under ECKANKAR in your phone book for an ECKANKAR Center near you. Or write: ECKANKAR, Att: Information, P.O. Box 27300, Minneapolis, MN 55427 U.S.A.

There May Be an
ECKANKAR Study Group near You

ECKANKAR offers a variety of local and international activities for the spiritual seeker. With hundreds of study groups worldwide, ECKANKAR is near you! Many areas have ECKANKAR Centers where you can browse through the books in a quiet, unpressured environment, talk with others who share an interest in this ancient teaching, and attend beginning discussion classes on how to gain the attributes of Soul: wisdom, power, love, and freedom.

Around the world, ECKANKAR study groups offer special one-day or weekend seminars on the basic teachings of ECKANKAR. Check your phone book under **ECKANKAR**, or call **(612) 544-0066** for membership informa-tion and the location of the ECKANKAR Center or study group nearest you. Or write **ECKANKAR, Att: Information, P.O. Box 27300, Minneapolis, MN 55427 U.S.A.**

☐ Please send me information on the nearest ECKANKAR discussion or study group in my area.

☐ Please send me more information about membership in ECKANKAR, which includes a twelve-month spiritual study.

Please type or print clearly   941

Name _____

Street _____ Apt. # _____

City _____ State/Prov._____

Zip/Postal Code _____ Country _____